BLACK MONDAYS

BLACK MONDAYS

Worst
Decisions
of the
Supreme
Court

Joel D. Joseph

A
ZENITH
EDITION

NATIONAL PRESS
Bethesda, Maryland

Cover by Barry Moyer.

Library of Congress Cataloging-in-Publication Data

Joseph, Joel D.
Black Mondays

Includes index.

1. United States-Constitutional law-Cases.
2. Civil Rights-United States-Cases
3. United States. Supreme Court.
I. Title
KF4549.J67 1987   347.73'26   87-14051
347.30735

ISBN 0-915765-65-9

PRINTED IN THE UNITED STATES OF AMERICA

Second Edition

Dedication

This book is dedicated to citizens who have been deprived of their constitutional rights, especially those who have stubbornly pursued their rights and the rights of others.

━━━━━━━━━━━━━━

Acknowledgments

The author thanks Ayfer Jafri for her outstanding editorial assistance and George E. Perry for his in-depth research. The author also acknowledges the assistance of the following individuals and organizations: American Civil Liberties Union, Professor Chester Antieau, Scott Atlas, Bruce Boraas, Jack Breard, Jr., Carroll County Historical Society, Walter Chaplinski, Harold Chernock, Circuit Court of Carroll County, Maryland, Sarisse Creighton, Arthur Eisenberg, Irving Feiner, Ralph Ginzburg, William Gobitas, Michael Hardwick, Fred Korematsu, Richard Kupfer, Library of Congress, James McNamara, Justice Thurgood Marshall, Ernest Mathews, National Archives, Carl Neil, John Sheehy, Professor David Skover, James Stanley, Professor Clyde Summers, Supreme Court Watch, Don Tamaki, United States Supreme Court Library, Reason Warehime and Kathleen L. Wilde.

Table of Contents

Preface

The first edition of this book was published in 1987 on the 200th anniversary of the enactment of the Constitution of the United States. Next year marks the 200th birthday of the Bill of Rights, the first ten amendments to the Constitution. These ten amendments include our most important freedoms: freedom of speech, assembly, religion, association, privacy and fundamental criminal rights.

The Supreme Court may have made poor decisions in the past three years, but none are of the magnitude of the cases included in the first edition of this book. In fact, the nation's highest tribunal made several courageous decisions, including the flag burning decisions. The Court ruled that the First Amendment protected the right of protesters to burn the American flag. This decision was another of those five-to-four decisions (one vote would have changed the result), demonstrating the unpredictability of future court decisions. It was a difficult decision, and the result caused an uproar in Congress and at the White House, with people clamoring for a constitutional amendment to "protect" the flag.

This edition includes citations to recent decisions, so that readers will be able to research cases further. The reader should keep in mind that, although the Supreme Court upholds our most precious liberties in a majority of cases, we, as a Nation, must confront and understand mistakes that were made by the Court and attempt to avoid repeating these errors.

Foreword

by Justice Thurgood Marshall

Nineteen-eighty-seven marks the 200th anniversary of the United States Constitution. A commission has been established to coordinate the celebration. The official meetings, essay contests, and festivities have begun.

The planned commemoration will span three years, and I am told 1987 is "dedicated to the memory of the Founders and the document they drafted in Philadelphia."[1] We are to "recall the achievements of our Founders and the knowledge and experience that inspired them, the nature of the government they established, its origins, its character, and its ends, and the rights and privileges of citizenship, as well as its attendant responsibilities."[2]

Like many anniversary celebrations, the plan for 1987 takes particular events and holds them up as the source of all the very best that has followed. Patriotic feelings will surely swell, prompting proud proclamations of the wisdom, foresight, and sense of justice shared by the Framers and reflected in a written document now yellowed with age. This is unfortunate—not that patriotism itself, but the tendency for the celebration to oversimplify, and overlook the many other events that have been instrumental to our achievements as a nation. The focus of this celebration invites a complacent belief that the vision of those who debated and compromised in Philadelphia yielded the "more perfect Union" it is said we now enjoy.

I cannot accept this invitation, for I do not believe that the meaning of the Constitution was forever "fixed" at the Philadelphia Convention. Nor do I find the wisdom, foresight, and sense of justice exhibited by the Framers particularly profound. To the contrary, the government they devised was defective from the start, requiring several amendments, a civil war, and momentous social transformation to attain the system of constitutional government, and its respect for the individual freedoms and human rights, we hold as fundamental today. When contemporary Americans cite "The Constitution," they invoke a concept that is vastly different from what the Framers barely began to construct two centuries ago.

For a sense of the evolving nature of the Constitution we need look no further than the first three words of the document's preamble: "We the People." When the Founding Fathers used this phrase in 1787, they did not have in mind the majority of America's citizens. "We the People" included, in the words of the Framers, "the whole Number of free Persons."3 On a matter so basic as the right to vote, for example, Negro slaves were excluded, although they were counted for representational purposes—at three-fifths each. Women did not gain the right to vote for over a hundred and thirty years.[4]

These omissions were intentional. The record of the Framers' debates on the slave question is especially clear: The Southern States acceded to the demands of the New England States for giving Congress broad power to regulate commerce, in exchange for the right to continue the slave trade. The economic interests of the regions coalesced: New Englanders engaged in the "carrying trade" would profit from transporting slaves from Africa as well as goods produced in America by slave labor. The perpetuation of slavery ensured the primary source of wealth in the Southern States.

Despite this clear understanding of the role slavery would play in the new republic, use of the words "slaves" and "slavery" was carefully avoided in the original document. Political representation in the lower House of Congress was to be based on the population of "free Persons" in each State, plus three-fifths of all "other persons."[5] Moral principles against slavery, for those who had them, were compromised, with no explanation of the conflicting principles for which the American Revolutionary War has ostensibly been fought: the self-evident truths "that all men are created equal, that they are endowed by their Creator with certain unalienable Rights, that among these are Life, Liberty and the pursuit of Happiness."[6]

It was not the first such compromise. Even these ringing phrases from the Declaration of Independence are filled with irony, for an early draft of what became that Declaration assailed the King of England for and for encouraging slave rebellions.[7] The final draft adopted in 1776 did not contain this criticism. And so again at the Constitutional Convention eloquent objections to the institution of slavery went unheeded, and its opponents eventually consented to a document which laid a foundation for the tragic events that were to follow.

Pennsylvania's Gouverneur Morris provides an example. He opposed slavery and the counting of slave in determining the basis for representation in Congress. At the Convention he objected that:

> "the inhabitant of Georgia (or) South Carolina who goes to the coast of Africa, and in defiance of the most sacred laws of humanity tears away his fellow creatures from their dearest connections and damns them to the most cruel bondages, shall have more votes in a Government instituted for the protection of the rights of mankind, than the Citizen of Pennsylvania or New Jersey who views with a laudable horror, so nefarious a practice."[8]

And yet Gouverneur Morris eventually accepted the three-fifths accommodation. In fact, he wrote the final draft of the Constitution, the very document the bicentennial will commemorate.

As a result of the compromise, the right of the Southern States to continue importing slaves was extended, officially, at least until 1808. We know that it actually lasted a good deal longer, as the Framers possessed no monopoly on the ability to trade moral principles for self-interest. But they nevertheless set an unfortunate example. Slaves could be imported, if the commerical interests of the North were protected. To make the compromise even more palatable, customs duties would be imposed at up to ten dollars per slave as a means of raising public revenues.[9]

No doubt it will be said, when the unpleasant truth of the history of slavery in America is mentioned during this bicentennial year, that the Constitution was a product of its times, and embodied a compromise which, under other circumstances, would not have been made. But the effects of the Framers' compromise have remained for generations. They arose from the contradiction between guaranteeing liberty and justice to all, and denying both to Negroes.

The original intent of the phrase, "We the People," was far too clear for any ameliorating construction. Writing for the Supreme Court in 1857, Chief Justice Taney penned the following passage in the *Dred Scott* case,[10] on the issue whether, in the eyes of the Framers, slaves were "constituent members of the sovereignty," and were to be included among "We the People":

> We think they are not, and that they are not included, and were not intended to be included .... They had for more than a century before been regarded as beings of an inferior order, and altogether unfit to associate with the white race ... ; and so far inferior, that they had no rights

which the white man was bound to
respect; and that the negro might justly
and lawfully be reduced to slavery for
his benefit . . . . (A)ccordingly, a negro
of the African race was regarded . . . as
an article of property, and held, and
bought and sold as such . . . . (N)o one
seems to have doubted the correctness of
the prevailing opinion of the time."

And so, nearly seven decades after the Constitutional
Convention, the Supreme Court reaffirmed the
prevailing opinion of the Framers regarding the rights
of Negroes in America. It took a bloody civil war
before the 13th Amendment would be adopted to
abolish slavery, though not the consequences slavery
would have for future Americans.

While the Union survived the civil war, the
Constitution did not. In its place arose a new, more
promising basis for justice and equality, the 14th
Amendment, ensuring protection of the life, liberty,
and property of *all* persons against deprivations without
due process, and guaranteeing equal protection of the
laws. And yet almost another century would pass
before any significant recognition was obtained of the
rights of black Americans to share equally even in
such basic opportunities as education, housing, and
employment, and to have their votes counted, and
counted equally. In the meantime, blacks joined
America's military to fight its wars and invested untold
hours working in its factories and on its farms,
contributing to the development of this country's
magificent wealth and waiting to share in its prosperity.

What is striking is the role legal principles have played throughout America's history in determining the conditions of Negroes. They were enslaved by law, emancipated by law, disenfranchised by law and segregated by law; and finally they have begun to win equality by law. Along the way, new constitutional principles have emerged to meet the challenges of a changing society. The progress has been dramatic, and it will continue.

The men who gathered in Philadelphia in 1787 could not have envisioned these changes. They could not have imagined, nor would they have accepted, that the document they were drafting would one day be construed by a Supreme Court to which had been appointed a woman and the descendent of an African slave. "We the People" no longer enslave, but the credit does not belong to the Framers. It belongs to those who refused to acquiesce in the outdated notions of "liberty," "justice," and "equality," and who strived to better them.

And so we must be careful, when focusing on the events which took place in Philadelphia two centuries ago, that we not overlook the momentous events which followed, and thereby lose our proper sense of perspective. Otherwise, the odds are that for many Americans the bicentennial celebration will be little more than a blind pilgrimage to the shrine of the original document now stored in a vault in the National Archives. If we seek, instead, a sensitive understanding of the Constitution's inherent defects, and its promising evolution through 200 years of history, the celebration of the "Miracle at Philadelphia"[11] will, in my view, be a far more meaningful and humbling experience. We will see that the true miracle was not the birth of the Constitution, buts its life, a life nurtured through two turbulent centuries of our own making, and a life embodying much good fortune that was not.

Thus, in this bicentennial year, we may not all participate in the festivities with flag-waving fervor. Some may more quietly commemorate the suffering, struggle, and sacrifice that has triumphed over much of what was wrong with the original document, and observe the anniversary with hopes not realized and promises not fulfilled. I plan to celebrate the bicentennial of the Constitituion as a living document, including the Bill of Rights and the other amendments protecting individual freedoms and human rights.

May, 1987

Footnotes to Foreword

1. *Commission on the Bicentennial of the United States Constitution, First Full Year's Report*, at 7 (September 1986).

2. *Ibid*, at 6.

3. *United States Constitution*, Art. 1, Section 2 (September 17, 1787).

4. The 19th Amendment (ratified in 1920).

5. *United States Constitution*, Art. 1, Section 2 (September 17, 1787)

6. *Declaration of Independence (July 4, 1776)*.

7. *See Becker, The Declaration of Independence: A Study in the History of Political Ideas* 147 (1942).

8. Farrant, ed., *The Records of the Federal Convention of 1787*, vol. II, 222 (New Haven, Conn., 1911).

9. *United States Constitution*, Art. 1, Section 9 (September 17, 1787).

10. 19 How. (60 U.S.) 393, 405, 407-408 (1857).

11. Bowen, *Miracle at Philadelphia: The Story of the Constitutional Convention May to September* 1787 (Boston, 1966).

Chapter One

Introduction

"We have long suffered under base prostitution of law to party passions in one judge, and the imbecility of another."

—Thomas Jefferson

The Constitution of the United States was, and as amended is, an excellent document. It is the oldest written constitution still in force in the world and has been used as a model for the constitutions of many other nations.

Although I generally agree with the views of Justice Marshall, expressed in his opinions and expressed in the foreword to this book, I disagree with his view that the Constitution was defective from the start. Of course it had defects. Some of the major defects were quickly corrected by passing the first ten amendments known as the Bill of Rights in 1791, just two years after the Constitution went into effect. The First Amendment, which includes the right to free speech and the right to freedom of religion, was light years ahead of the standards of other nations at the time, and is still far ahead of the standards of human rights throughout most of the world today.

Most of the problems cited by Justice Marshall stem from those whose duty it is to interpret the Constitution: the nine justices of the Supreme Court, and not from the document itself.

For example, Justice Marshall cites *Dred Scott v. Sandford* in his foreword. In that case the Supreme Court ruled that slaves and former slaves were not citizens of the United States. Justice Marshall blames the Framers of the Constitution for the *Dred Scott* decision (see chapter twelve).

However, nowhere in the Constitution does it state that Americans of African descent are not citizens of the United States. The Constitution defines "We the People" of the United States as the number of "free Persons" residing in the States. Slavery was recognized in the Constitution as part of a compromise to form this nation. In the document slaves were to be counted as three-fifths of a free person for the purposes of representation in Congress. However, at the time the Constitution was written there were a significant number of Negro free Persons. These citizens were allowed to vote. The Supreme Court should have recognized free African-Americans as citizens.

The majority of the Supreme Court who ruled in the *Dred Scott* case were from the slave states, and their biases and prejudices shaped the opinion that they wrote. I blame the members of the Supreme Court for the *Dred Scott* decision, not the Constitution. Although we are a nation of laws, not men, it takes men (and women) to interpret those laws. The Supreme Court's erroneous decision in the *Dred Scott* case, not the Constitution, led to the War Between the States.

Concerning women's rights, Justice Marshall implied that the Constitution was defective in that it denied women the right to vote. Nowhere in the Constitution does it state that only men have the right to vote. As with the rights of Negroes, the Supreme Court, with no constitutional basis, unanimously ruled in 1875 that women did not have the right to vote (see chapter sixteen). And that was after the Fourteenth Amendment, with its equal protection clause, was enacted. It took the Nineteenth Amendment, which overturned that decision of the Supreme Court, to clarify the Constitution and to mandate that women have the right to vote.

I agree with Justice Marshall that too much effort is now being spent waving the flag and printing the Constitution on fast food placemats. The major thrust of this book is to examine the worst twenty or so decisions of the Supreme Court, out of thousands of cases, so that we can avoid making similar mistakes in the future.

Black Mondays

The title to this book was selected because most of the Supreme Court's decisions are announced on Monday. This has been so for most of the court's history. In recent years, however, the court's backlog has made it necessary to issue some decisions on other days of the week.

Criteria for Selection of Cases

Numerous associations and law professors were asked for nominations of the Supreme Court's "worst decisions." In order to qualify for inclusion in this book, a case had to be poorly reasoned and also had to have a major impact on the freedoms of American citizens. In a few cases the Supreme Court admitted that it had erred in its decision in an earlier case. In others, such as the *Japanese Internment* case (see chapter fifteen), later actions of Congress and overseas reactions make it clear that the decision was overruled by the "court of history."

Most cases never reach the Supreme Court. Many of the worst decisions of courts come at the lowest levels. Many of those cases are not appealed. And the Supreme Court declines to review thousands of cases every year. Although a denial of review can be a horrendous decision, I only considered cases when the Supreme Court granted review and issued an opinion in a case. Hundreds of cases were considered and the list was narrowed to twenty-four.

Most of the cases selected for inclusion in this book had strong dissenting opinions. Some were close cases (five to four) and very few were unanimous. The unanimous decisions tended to rely on a series of earlier cases where the court tended not to focus on the express language of the Constitution.

What Potter Stewart said of pornography—he could not define it but "knew it when he saw it"—applies to an attempt to define the worst decisions. Both are in the minds of the readers. One man's pornography is another man's art. What is a bad decision for one person is good for another.

Concerning the pornography decisions of the court, unlike other areas of law, it was very difficult to single out one case that was especially loathsome. For much of the twentieth century, the Supreme Court has struggled without success to define pornography and to exclude it from First Amendment protection. Every decade the Court tinkers with its definition, as it has done again this year. Justice Douglas opposed all of these definitions and felt that until there was a constitutional amendment concerning the regulation of pornography, the court should not become the censor of last resort. Justice Stewart, although opposing "hardcore pornography," felt that the worst Supreme Court decision during his tenure was the *Ginzburg* censorship case. Many other "obscenity" cases could have also been included.

Research Techniques

In addition to the traditional sources for legal research, I interviewed the parties and attorneys to most of the cases in this book. This was done in an attempt to add flesh to the bare facts of the cases, to bring them to life. These interviews filled in missing facts unavailable elsewhere, including what had happened to the parties after the decisions by the Supreme Court. Concerning the older cases, where all of the parties and attorneys are deceased, old newspapers, magazines, archives and other sources were used.

Organization

The cases in this book are divided into six parts. Freedom of Religion is the first, and although none of the cases in that part involve anyone going to jail or suffering an atrocious injustice, nevertheless the fundamental principle of religious tolerance is violated. Freedom of religion is one fundamental right which sets the United States apart from many other nations, including England, and is one reason that many sought refuge in this country.

The second part includes two cases involving freedom of association and the right to privacy. The cases involve the right to choose your roommates, and the right to privacy in your bedroom. The third part includes seven freedom of speech cases. The cases are quite varied, involving disputes concerning "fighting words", "dirty words", unpopular speakers, going door-to-door, freedom of speech in shopping malls and the right to protest against the Soviet Union. The first three parts of the book stem from rights enumerated in the First Amendment, which, to a large extent, separates free countries from totalitarian regimes.

Part Four covers equal protection of the law. It includes the landmark civil rights cases as well as some lesser-known discrimination decisions. Few Americans are aware that the Supreme Court, not the Constitution, denied women the right to vote over a hundred years ago. The Japanese Internment case is also included in this part.

The fifth part, concerned with criminal rights, includes three cases. These cases involved the right to counsel, cruel and unusual punishment and the presumption of innocence. The court held that it was not cruel or unusual to sentence a man to life imprisonment for stealing $229.11 in three non-violent crimes.

The last part of the book deals with access to justice. Four cases are included, two concerning the rights of veterans. The court denied plaintiffs in these cases the right to sue or granted defendant immunity from suit. Immunity from suit was granted to the Army, the FBI and judges, even though the constitutional rights of the plaintiffs were violated.

This book does not have to be read in order. If women's rights, or civil rights, or free speech interest you most, read those cases first. The last part of the book contains some of the most compelling cases, so it should not be missed.

Why Good Courts Make Bad Decisions

Even the best courts occasionally make bad decisions. Many bad decisions are made during national emergencies, especially during war time. It was during the chaos of World War II that the court approved the internment of American citizens of Japanese descent. Ironically, one of the advocates of internment, Earl Warren, became, in my opinion, one of the best chief justices of the Supreme Court.

Another reason for poor decisions is that the courts sometimes rely on history to make decisions for them.

For example, the court will say, "this practice has gone unchallenged for 150 years." Or the court will rely on early decisions which rely on an earlier decision. So what! One early case can breed hundreds of clones all resting on one lousy, albeit early, decision. The separate but equal cases were built up this way.

In a related manner the court will often get wound up in its own line of cases on a particular subject. For example, in the *Soviet Boycott* case (see chapter eleven) the court followed its line of labor law cases on secondary boycotts and lost sight of the constitutional rights of citizens. In that case the court unanimously ruled that American longshoremen could not boycott Soviet ships in protest against the Russian invasion of Afghanistan. That is the only case in this book where I parted company with Justice Marshall. The next time the court examines a clash between our labor laws and the right to free speech and association, perhaps the First Amendment will prevail.

Amending the Constitution

Because the Framers knew that the Constitution was not perfect, they built in an amendment process. The Framers recognized that the compromises which were struck in 1787 would not last forever. The amendment process was made intentionally difficult. After the Bill of Rights was enacted we have had less than one amendment per decade.

If the Constitution is to be perfected it has to be carefully amended. One major problem with the document that no judge will point out is that the Constitution gives federal judges life tenure. In theory this makes judges independent. In reality it keeps inept judges on the bench. Currently, the only way to remove a federal judge is by Congressional impeachment.

Life expectancy has increased dramatically since the Constitution was enacted. A life appointment made then might have meant a fifteen-year judgeship. Now it can be a forty-year appointment, or more. A Constitutional amendment providing for judicial terms of ten years (with five years of additional salary for retirement or for a buffer period) would give judges independence while instituting new energy into the judiciary. An excellent judge could serve ten years at the district court level, ten at the appellate level, and ten at the Supreme Court. No judge would be allowed to be reappointed at the lower two levels. At the Supreme Court reappointment would be reasonable because the Senate exercises careful monitoring of the highest court.

Most observers will agree that the electoral college needs amending. The two-year term of members of Congress is also the target of many who want to amend the document. The principle of "one person, one vote" is violated by an early constitutional compromise: the United States Senate. It is undemocratic that New York State should get only two senators while Wyoming and Hawaii (not admitted to the Union until relatively recently and not parties to the original compromise) and other sparsely populated states should get the same number of senators. I propose that the Senate be kept to one hundred members, and that each state get at least one. However, the other fifty Senate seats should be appointed by population. New York may get eight, Illinois five and Delaware one. The senators would still represent their states at large, but larger states would get a new senator more often. There is no longer any justification for this oddity in our Constitution.

Conclusion

I hope that this book will cause citizens, students, lawyers, and judges to think about our Constitution. Since the amendment process was built in to it, it is not made out of stone. I also hope that this book will cause the nation to turn its attention to the quality of our judges at all levels.

PART 1
Freedom of Religion

Chapter Two

The Day of Rest

"Congress shall make no law respecting an establishment of religion, or prohibiting the free exercise thereof."

—First Amendment

Springfield, Massachusetts has only a small Jewish population. However, beginning in 1953 it supported the Crown Kosher Super Market, at 57 Sumner Avenue. Orthodox Jews from as far away as Vermont and Connecticut shopped in Harold Chernock's market because their small towns did not have a purveyor of kosher foods. The closest kosher supermarket was twenty-six miles away in Hartford, Connecticut.

Because Mr. Chernock and other owners of the store were Orthodox Jews, the Crown market closed at sundown on Friday night and did not reopen until Sunday morning. Observance of the Jewish sabbath required this practice. More than one-third of Crown's business took place on Sundays.

Crown Kosher Supermarket during the 1960s, courtesy of Harold Chernock.

The Lord's Day

Massachusetts had a Sunday closing law called the "Lord's Day Statute" which required most stores to be closed on Sunday. The Massachusetts law was originally enacted in 1653, more than a hundred years before the U.S. Constitution was ratified. The early law undeniably had a religious purpose, to compel observance of the Christian sabbath. Although the law had been amended over the 300-year period, it remained in effect in the twentieth century.

The Law provided:

> "Whoever on the Lord's day keeps open his shop, warehouse or workhouse, or

does any manner of labor, business or work, except works of necessity and charity, shall be punished by a fine of fifty dollars."

On May 2nd, May 30th and June 6th, 1954 (all Sundays), members of the Springfield Police Department went to the Crown Market and made purchases of food items. Based on those "illegal" sales three criminal complaints were filed against Mr. Chernock. He was tried and convicted of violating the "Lord's Day Statute" on June 15th, 1954 and was fined forty-five dollars.

Raymond P. Gallagher, the Chief of Police of Springfield, threatened to continue to enforce the "Lord's Day" law. To prevent this harassment, the Crown Kosher Super Market and three of its customers sued Mr. Gallagher in Federal Court in Boston. The Chief Rabbi of Massachusetts joined them in the case. They argued that the Sunday closing law violated the First Amendment's principles of separation of church and state. The Supreme Court had earlier ruled that the First Amendment applied to the states as well as to the Federal Government.

In Federal Court

The federal court sitting in Boston ruled that the Lord's Day Statute was unconstitutional and enjoined the Chief of Police from enforcing it. The panel of three judges ruled against the validity of the law by a two to one vote with Judge McCarthy dissenting. The Commonwealth of Massachusetts appealed to the United States Supreme Court. While the appeal progressed Crown continued to open on Sundays.

The Supreme Court

On Monday, May 29th, 1961, the Supreme Court ruled six to three that the Massachusetts law did not violate the constitutional provision which separates church and state.[1] The court found that, although the origins of the law were undoubtedly religious, its purpose had become secular. A day of rest, claimed the court, is good for people, and the idea of a day of rest need not have religious implications. Further, the court argued, the day of rest should be uniform for all members of the society.

The Supreme Court's decision is wrong because a truly secular law could have exempted stores like Crown. The law had seventy exceptions, allowing stores to sell tobacco, ice cream, milk, bread, live bait for fishing, and newspapers. With all of these exceptions, why not have one more for kosher food stores? Or, why not allow stores to close on one day other than Sunday?

Even if it is granted that a day of rest is a good thing, why must everyone rest on the same day? The "Lord's Day Statute" allowed the Boston Celtics to play basketball, the Bruins to play hockey and the Red Sox baseball. Don't professional athletes need a day of rest also? Why should a law permit Larry Bird of the Celtics to pound a basketball while forbidding a kosher butcher from chopping meat? What great harm would have come to Springfield had Crown been allowed to open on Sunday? Considerable harm could come, however, to a small grocery store forced to stay closed on Sunday, the only day Orthodox Jewish customers who work on weekdays are able to do their shopping.

Freedom of religion is one of the fundamental rights provided in the Constitution. Religious persecution forced many people to seek asylum in the United States. Yet the Supreme Court turned a deaf ear to religious tolerance and showed its insensitivity to the concept of separation of church and state.

Three justices dissented. One of them, Justice William O. Douglas, said:

> "The question is whether a State can impose criminal sanctions on those who, unlike the Christian majority that makes up our society, worship on a different day or do not share the religious scruples of the majority.
>
> *   *   *
>
> If the 'free exercise' of religion were subject to reasonable regulation, as it is under some constitutions, or if all laws "respecting establishment of religion" were not proscribed, I could understand how rational men, representing a predominantly Christian civilization, might think that Sunday laws did not unreasonably interfere with anyone's free exercise of religion.

*   *   *

I dissent from applying criminal sanctions
against any of the complainants since to
do so implicates the state in religious
matters contrary to the constitutional
mandate."

Justice Stewart joined Justice Douglas in dissent. He
remarked:

"Massachusetts has passed a law which
compels an Orthodox Jew to choose
between his religious faith and his
economic survival. That is a cruel choice.
It is a choice which I think no State can
constitutionally demand. For me this is
not something that can be swept under
the rug and forgotten in the interest of
Sunday togetherness. I think the impact
of this law on these "religious men"
grossly violates their constitutional right
to free exercise of their religion."

A majority of the court forgot a warning issued during the Congressional discussion of the First Amendment:[2]

"The rights of conscience are, in their nature, of particular delicacy, and will bear
the gentlest touch of governmental hand."

Freedom of thought and religion are fundamental
freedoms. It can be argued that they are even more
fundamental than free speech, because the free exercise
of these rights has virtually no impact on others.
Thought and religion are most often in the mind of the

believer, while speech by its very nature thrusts itself at others.

Epilogue

The year after the Supreme Court's decision the Commonwealth of Massachusetts changed its "Lord's Day Statute" to allow the Crown Market to open for business on Sundays.

Crown Kosher Super Market stayed in business for twenty-four years, from 1953 until 1979. In 1979 Harold Chernock sold the building that housed the market to the Friendly Ice Cream Company, and retired. Friendly's tore down the market and built one of its restaurants on the site.

Endnotes

1. *Gallagher v. Crown Kosher Super Market*, 366 U.S. 617 (1961).
2. *I: Annals of Congress*, 730 (remarks of Rep. Daniel Carroll of Maryland, August 15th, 1789).

Chapter Three

Freedom of Thought

"If there is any principle of the Constitution that more imperatively calls for attachment than any other it is the principle of free thought—not free thought for those who agree with us but freedom for the thought that we hate."

—Oliver Wendell Holmes

The Flag Salute Case

Minersville, Pennsylvania, a small town of some 10,000 souls in eastern Pennsylvania midway between Harrisburg and Wilkes-Barre, was founded in 1831. True to its name, coal mining is the principle industry in the town.

One afternoon in the Depression year of 1936 Lillian Gobitas, age twelve, and her brother William, age ten, were sent home from school. The principal of the school had told the Gobitas children that they could not attend the Minersville schools any more unless they agreed to salute the American flag at the opening exercises each morning.

Other children, along with their teachers, repeated the Pledge of Allegiance without objection. The Gobitas children refused to salute the flag because of their religious upbringing. The Gobitas family belonged to the Jehovah's Witnesses faith. They took the Ten Commandments literally and believed that when a person salutes a flag, any flag, he was bowing down before a graven image. Walter and Ruth Gobitas told their children that their religion prohibited them from saying the Pledge of Allegiance and saluting the flag at school or anywhere else.

The Minersville Board of Education placed the Pledge of Allegiance and the flag salute in the daily public school program. They believed that this would promote patriotism and good citizenship. The Gobitas family did not ask that the ceremony be abolished, only that children be excused from the ceremony if they had an objection to it.

The members of the Minersville Board of Education discussed the issue and could not see how saluting the flag could hurt any American child. The board included the town's leading citizens, doctors, and businessmen. The board declined to make an exception for the Gobitas children and directed the Superintendent of Schools, Charles Roudabush, to expel the children. Roudabush followed the board's directive.

Rather than having his children violate their religious faith, Walter Gobitas took Lillian and William out of the public school and enrolled them in Jones Kingdom School, a private school in the nearby town of Andreas, Pennsylvania. The Gobitas family was not poor but could not really afford the private school expenses.

Reluctant Plaintiff

Mr. Gobitas discussed his dilemma with members of his church. They advised him to discuss the matter with the American Civil Liberties Union. Walter Gobitas regretted that he had to file suit against the school board, but believed it was the right thing to do. He sued on behalf of his children, and on his own behalf, to be relieved of the financial burden of sending his children to private school. He emphasized that the laws of Pennsylvania made attendance at school compulsory, while at the same time the local school board had expelled his children for practicing their religion.

The school board, on the other hand, argued simply that it is proper to instill patriotism and a sense of country in schoolchildren and that the right of the Minersville schools to do so should override the children's religious rights.

William and Lillian Gobitas with their father Walter.

The case was assigned to Judge Albert Maris in the federal court in Philadelphia. Maris was a new judge, having just been appointed to the court by President Franklin D. Roosevelt. Judge Maris ruled in favor of the Gobitas family:

> "The refusal of Lillian and William to salute the flag in the Minersville Public School was based solely upon their sincerely held religious convictions that the act was forbidden by the express command of God as set forth in the Bible.
>
> *   *   *
>
> The enforcement of defendants' regulation requiring the flag salute by children who are sincerely opposed to it upon conscientious religious grounds is not a reasonable method of teaching civics, including loyalty to the State and Federal Government, but tends to have the contrary effect upon such children."

Judge Maris ordered the school board to pay $3,200 to the Gobitas family to reimburse them for the expense of private schooling. In addition he issued a restraining order requiring the school to reinstate the Gobitas children, and prohibited the school from requiring them to salute the flag and say the Pledge of Allegiance.

The School Board's Appeal

The Board of Education couldn't stomach Judge Maris' order. They voted to appeal the decision to the court of appeals. Apparently the board had to justify its earlier decisions which had cost the community a tidy sum for attorneys' fees, in addition to the award against it.

In 1939 the Third Circuit Court of Appeals in Philadelphia issued its decision. The three-judge panel was unanimous in its decision against the school board. Judge Clark wrote the opinion of the court, castigating Pennsylvania and seventeen other large states with flag salute policies. According to the court, some 120 students had been victimized by their policies.

Judge Clark compared the policy of these large states to those of Adolf Hitler, who at the same time had said that Jehovah's Witnesses were quacks and that all of their literature should be confiscated. The court concluded that the Board of Education of Minersville violated the basic principles upon which the Commonwealth of Pennsylvania was founded. Judge Clark said:

> "The state was colonized by William Penn. He came to the new country because his refusal to subordinate religious scruples to educational coercion led to his expulsion from Oxford University in the old."

The Supreme Court

The Board of Education appealed Judge Clark's ruling to the United States Supreme Court. The highest court agreed to hear the case. On behalf of the school board Joseph W. Henderson, a Philadelphia lawyer, argued the case before the Supreme Court. George K. Gardner of Boston, a Harvard Law School professor, argued on behalf of Mr. Gobitas and his children. A team of ACLU lawyers joined Professor Gardner in handling the case. The American Bar Association, which ordinarily avoids taking a position on pending cases, submitted a brief on behalf of the Gobitas family. The brief stated: "We suggest that no American court should presume to tell any person that he is wrong in his opinion as to how he may best serve the God in which he believes." The Bar Association added that there is no public need for compulsory flag salute.

Despite all of the legal talent and arguments made for the Gobitas family, on Monday, June 3rd, 1940 the Supreme Court ruled eight to one against them. Justice Felix Frankfurter, a Jewish immigrant from Vienna, Austria, wrote the opinion for the court. The court decided that it should not interfere with the authority of the local school board, and that, indeed, schoolchildren should be instilled with a sense of patriotism. Justice Stone wrote the lone dissenting opinion. On the day the decision was announced Justice Frankfurter, although expected to read his opinion, merely stated the result. Justice Stone, however, was so agitated by the case that he read his dissent in full. He said the mandatory flag salute

"does more than suppress freedom of

speech and more than prohibit the free exercise of religion . . . . For by this law the state seeks to coerce these children to express a sentiment which, as they interpret it, they do not entertain, and which violates their deepest religious convictions."

Public Reaction

The large-scale reaction of the media and the American people was an unusual response to a Supreme Court decision. More than 170 leading newspapers strongly criticized the decision, while only a handful supported it. The *St. Louis Post-Dispatch* said:

"We think its decision is a violation of American principle. We think it is a surrender to popular hysteria. If patriotism depends upon such things as this—upon a violation of a fundamental right of religious freedom, then it becomes not a noble emotion of love for country, but something to be rammed down our throats by the law."

Soon after the decision was handed down a rash of violent episodes victimized Jehovah's Witnesses around the country. A Jehovah's Witnesses Kingdom Hall was burned in Kennebunkport, Maine. A meeting of Witnesses in Rockville, Maryland was attacked. The lawyer for a group of Jehovah's Witnesses in Connorsville, Indiana was beaten and driven from town. In Litchfield, Illinois a caravan of Witnesses' cars was overturned.

In Minersville, the Gobitas family received threatening phone calls telling them to get out of town. Citizens boycotted Mr. Gobitas' grocery store. The boycott, in addition to private school expenses, put a tremendous financial strain on the Gobitas family.

In many states flag salute regulations were strictly enforced, many Jehovah's Witnesses were expelled, and some were sent to reform school.

In 1941 West Virginia passed a compulsory flag salute law. Three Jehovah's Witnesses students who were expelled from school filed suit in Charleston, West Virginia. Their case worked its way to the Supreme Court rapidly. By 1943 the court was ready to make its decision.

During the three years between the *Gobitis*[1] case to *West Virginia State Board of Education v. Barnette*, the composition of the Supreme Court had changed dramatically. Justices McReynolds and Hughes had retired. Justice Stone was elevated to Chief Justice and Robert Jackson and James Byrnes were appointed to the bench. In the meantime Justices Black, Douglas, and Murphy distanced themselves from the *Gobitis* decision.

The Supreme Court handed down its ruling on Flag Day, Monday, June 14th, 1943. In three years the Supreme Court made its quickest and most complete reversal in its history. The court ruled six to three, directly overruling the *Gobitis* decision. Justice Jackson wrote a virulent majority opinion; Justice Frankfurter wrote a bitter dissenting opinion.

Epilogue

The Gobitas children graduated from private schools and then moved to Brooklyn, New York to work at Watchtower, the national headquarters of the Jehovah's Witnesses. William Gobitas worked there for ten years. He met his future wife and moved to her hometown near Milwaukee, Wisconsin, where he now resides. His three daughters attended the Waubeka-Freedonia schools and were not required to pledge allegiance to the flag. After working for an insurance company for twenty years, Mr. Gobitas took early retirement in 1976.

Lillian Gobitas met her future husband, Irwin Klose, while working at the Watchtower. Mr. Klose, also a Jehovah's Witness, escaped from Nazi Germany, where Witnesses had been put into concentration camps along with Jews and other "misfits" of society. The Kloses now reside in a suburb of Atlanta, Georgia.

Issues concerning the American flag continue to grab the attention of politicians and the American people. During the 1988 presidential campaign, Vice President Bush attacked Governor Michael Dukakis' position in a Massachusetts controversy in which the governor sided with teachers who did not want to lead students in reciting the pledge of allegiance.

During the 1984 Republican convention, Gregory Johnson burned an American flag in protest against the Reagan administration. Johnson was arrested and charged with desecration of the American flag. In 1989 the Supreme Court, in a five-to-four decision, ruled that Johnson had a constitutional right to burn the American flag as political protest protected by the First Amendment. President Bush and many other pushed for a constitutional amendment to "protect" the flag. Congress would not support a constitutional amendment and passed a federal statute as a compromise. On June 11, 1990 in *United States v. Eichman,* the Supreme Court ruled this new statute unconstitutional. Once again the President raised the specter of a constitutional amendment, but at this time it looks like a lot of flag-waiving for political gain.

An Officer and a Gentleman

Clyde Summers was born on a farm in Grass Range, Montana in 1918. His family moved to Tecumseh, Nebraska for a while and then settled in Winchester, Illinois when Clyde was eleven. It was 1929, the year of the stock market crash, and the year that his mother had died. The Summers family remained in Illinois where Clyde Summers went to high school and then college. He earned a bachelor of science degree in accounting at the University of Illinois and then graduated from the University's law school in 1942 with honors. It was war time and Summers' brother was in the Army.

Clyde Summers was a religious man. He regularly attended services at the Methodist Church and led worship services at school. He worked his way through college doing kitchen work, washing windows, and running elevators. The university hired him to work in the accounting office. He didn't have any dates with girls during the first three years at college because he didn't have the money and he was too busy studying and working.

Clyde Wilson Summers while his case was before the Supreme Court, courtesy of Professor Summers.

Because of deeply held religious beliefs Clyde Summers was opposed to war. Summers did not drink or smoke. He didn't even dance because he did not believe in it. He believed in non-violent resistance like that of Mahatma Gandhi. He registered as a conscientious objector and the Illinois Draft Board accepted his beliefs as genuine, classifying him as a 4- E, a conscientious objector, not to be drafted for the armed forces. He failed his physical examination, so he would not have been drafted for this reason either.

Character and Fitness

Mr. Summers took the Illinois bar exam in June of 1942. He passed and applied for admission to practice law. Walter Bellatti, a member of the committee on character and fitness, questioned Clyde's fitness to practice law. On November 27th, 1942, Summers appeared before the full committee on character and fitness and was questioned at length.

> Q: Mr. Summers, is there any question in your mind as to whether you were cut out for a preacher or a music teacher rather than a lawyer?
>
> A: Sometimes I very seriously consider going into the ministry. The fact is I considered it through most of the two years of my schooling.
>
> Q: Why did you change your mind?
> A: Because I felt that there were enough religious people in the chur-

ches—I mean the ministry. I think there is a lot of work to be done in the law.

Q: Do you expect to use the law as a vehicle for the extension of your ideas?

A: That is not my purpose in law, just a means of getting at these things, but when the situation has come up in law that my principles guide me, I will follow them, whether it is in relation to non-violence or not. There is a lot of religion other than non-violence. I think there is work that needs to be done. A lot of prison reform that needs to be done. I think it is un-Christian the kind of prisons we have. I think there are a lot of other things that perhaps the law has a place to do.

I think that the law has a place to see to it that every man has a chance to eat and a chance to live equally. I think the law has a place where people can go and get justice done for themselves without paying too much, for the bulk of the people that are too poor. I have been particularly interested in the legal clinics that have been set up in different places. It is in the right direction.

Q: And is it in your opinion that an oath to support the Constitution of the United States would not oblige you to use force at any time? A: Military violent force.

Q: Or police force or individual physical force?

A: Yes.

Q: I cannot understand the distinction between military force and other force.

A: In the military you kill innocent people and in the other case you get the criminal.

On January 5th, 1943 Summers was advised that a majority of the committee on character and fitness declined to sign a favorable certificate as to his character and fitness. He was advised that the board of bar examiners would not certify him for admission to the bar without the certificate. No statement of the committee was supplied to him.

One member of the committee expressed his personal opinion:

"You eschew the use of force regardless of circumstances . . . . Your conduct is governed by a higher law which we all hope may someday prevail.

*   *   *

What protection can the law be to the weak if lawyers do not consider its mandate to be entitled to obedience by force if necessary[?] . . . [Y]our position seems inconsistent with the obligations of an attorney."

Appealing to the Supreme Court

Admission to the practice of law in Illinois is granted or denied by the Supreme Court of Illinois. Because his admission was denied Mr. Summers filed a petition with the United States Supreme Court seeking the review of the denial of his admission to practice.

While his petition was pending before the Supreme Court, Clyde Summers could not practice law. He was hired by the University of Toledo Law School as an instructor in law. Admission to a bar is not required for law professors or instructors.

The Highest Court Hands Down Its Decision

On June 11th, 1945, during the final chapters of World War II, the Supreme Court issued its ruling.[2] By the slimmest margin, five to four, the court ruled against Clyde Summers. It affirmed the right of the State of Illinois to decide what constituted fitness to practice law. It ruled that Illinois could deny Summers admission to the bar because of his deeply held belief that violence is contrary to the Bible. Illinois has a requirement that males between the ages of eighteen and forty-five serve in the militia in time of war, and because of this law Clyde Summers was declared unfit to practice law.

Justice Black dissented:

> "The State of Illinois has denied the petitioner the right to practice his profession and to earn a living as a lawyer. It has

denied him a license on the ground that his present religious beliefs disqualify him from membership in the legal profession. The question is, therefore, whether a state which requires a license as a prerequisite to practicing law can deny an applicant a license solely because of his deeply rooted religious convictions. The fact that the petitioner measures up to every other requirement for admission to the Bar by the State demonstrates beyond doubt that the only reason for his rejection was his religious beliefs.

*   *   *

The conclusion seems to me inescapable that if Illinois can bar this petitioner from the practice of law it can bar every person from every public occupation solely because he believes in non-resistance rather than in force. For a lawyer is not more subject to call for military duty than a plumber, a highway worker, a Secretary of State, or a prison chaplain.

*   *   *

Justice Holmes said that 'if there is any principle of the Constitution that more imperatively calls for attachment than any other it is the principle of free thought—not free thought for those who agree with us but freedom for the thought that we hate.' Under our Consti-

tution men are published for what they
do or fail to do and not for what they
think and believe."

Justice Black was joined in dissent by Justices
Douglas, Murphy, and Rutledge.

Epilogue

Clyde Wilson Summers has had a distinguished
career in law. After earning a masters degree in law,
and a doctorate in law from Columbia University, he
was admitted to practice law in New York in 1951. He
continued to teach at the University of Toledo Law
School until 1949, when he moved to the University of
Buffalo to teach law until 1957. After teaching at the
University of Buffalo, Summers taught at Yale University until 1975. Professor Summers currently teaches at
the University of Pennsylvania Law School.

Professor Summers is the author of five books on
labor law. He said the decision denying him admission
to the bar directed him toward teaching, which he
loves. His only practice of law concerned civil liberties
cases and draft cases.

Endnotes

1. *Minersville School District v. Gobitis,* 310 U.S. 589 (1940); the courts
misspelled the name Gobitas.
2. *In Re Summers,* 326 U.S. 561 (1945).

PART 2
Freedom of Association and the Right to Privacy

Chapter Four

Roommates

"Individuality is the salt of common life. You may have to live in a crowd but you do not have to live like it."

—Henry Van Dyke

Michael Truman, Bruce Boraas, Anne Parish and three other students at the State University of New York at Stony Brook together rented a six bedroom house in the Village of Belle Terre. Dr. Edwin and Judith Dickman owned the home that the group rented and approved of the students' living arrangements.

Michael Truman signed a lease with the Dickmans beginning December 31, 1971 and ending the following May, at $500 per month. And the end of the lease term the students could keep renting the property on a month-to-month basis. Bruce Boraas later co-signed the lease. None of the six students were related to each other. Each occupied one of the bedrooms and each paid a portion of the rent and other expenses. The group shared common kitchen facilities, dined together and paid common household expenses out of a "house" checking account. Four of the students were pursuing graduate studies in sociology at Stony Brook.

The group living arrangement was advantageous to the students because it kept their expenses down. In addition they enjoyed living together and it helped their studies because they could discuss sociology and other topics with their roommates.

The Village of Belle Terre

The Village of Belle Terre, which means "beautiful land" in French, consists of about 200 single-family homes, mostly built in the 1920s and 1930s, on large, wooded lots. Belle Terre has a town beach on Long Island Sound. Bruce Boraas and Michael Truman applied for village beach permits so that they could use the town beach during the summer. On June 8, 1972, the Village denied them permits because it considered the students to be illegal residents.

The Village is zoned exclusively for single-family houses. The zoning law limits the number of unrelated persons who can live together to two. People related by blood or marriage are not limited in a similar manner. A family with fourteen children could live together in one house, but three nuns could not legally live together in Belle Terre.

On July 19, 1972, the Village, after learning of the living arrangements of Boraas and Truman, served the Dickmans with a summons. On July 31st, the Dickmans were served with an "Order to Remedy Violations" concerning the living arrangements at their Belle Terre home. The order required the Dickmans to evict at least four of the students so that only two unrelated persons would be left in the home.

A Federal Case

On August 2nd, the New York Civil Liberties Union filed suit on behalf of the Dickmans and three of the students seeking to have the Belle Terre zoning law declared unconstitutional because it interfered with their freedom of association. The lawsuit was filed in federal court because it was based on federal civil rights laws and on the Constitution. The case was assigned to Judge Dooling, who promptly issued a temporary restraining order (TRO) against the village. This order restrained the village for ten days from enforcing the zoning ordinance against the group house.

Judge Dooling kept the TRO in force until he could hold a hearing on the matter. Following a hearing, on September 20, 1972, Judge Dooling issued a forty page decision denying a permanent injunction. He ruled that zoning ordinance was a valid exercise of the village's authority to control population density. However, he granted a five-day stay to allow the plaintiffs to file an appeal.

Lawyers for the students and the Dickmans filed an appeal with the Second Circuit Court of Appeals. The federal appeals court, by a vote of two to one, reversed the lower court ruling and reinstated the injunction against Belle Terre. Judge Mansfield ruled:

"The effect of the Belle Terre ordinance
would be to exclude from the community, without any rational basis, unmarried groups seeking to live together,
whether they be three college students,
three single nurses, three priests, or three
single judges."[1]

Before the Supreme Court

The Village of Belle Terre took the appeals court
ruling to the Supreme Court. The Supreme Court
agreed to review the case.

On April 1, 1974, the court issued its ruling. Justice
Douglas, usually the court's dissenting liberal, delivered
the opinion for the court:

"The ordinance places no ban on other
forms of association, for a 'family' may,
so far as the ordinance is concerned, entertain whomever it likes.

*   *   *

A quiet place where yards are wide,
people few, and motor vehicles restricted
are legitimate guidelines in a land-use
project addressed to family needs."[2]

Rarely does Justice William O. Douglas brush aside
freedom of association, but in this one case he sided
with the authority of localities to zone out certain

types of individuals. Douglas was a strong environmentalist and his bias in favor of environmental regulations must have contaminated his reasoning. His concern about controlling population density could have been dealt with by a village zoning ordinance which limited the number of persons living in a home to one person per bedroom, or to a certain number per house. The village could have also limited the number of automobiles per house in order to reduce traffic.

Justice Douglas said that the zoning ordinance "involves no 'fundamental' right guaranteed by the Constitution, such as voting, the right of association or any rights of privacy." What more fundamental right of association is there than determining who you choose to live with? Isn't the right to privacy violated when a town can inquire into who is living with whom? If two unmarried housemates have a friend stay with them for a week are they in violation of the zoning ordinance? What if the guest stays for two weeks, or a month, or six months? Do we want our city officials peeping into windows, or barging into our bedrooms to take notes as to whom is living with us? If this isn't part of our right to privacy then our right to privacy is meaningless.

Justices Brennan and Marshall dissented. Justice Marshall stated:

> "In my view, the disputed classification burdens the students' fundamental rights of association and privacy guaranteed by the First and Fourteenth Amendments.

*   *   *

Our decisions established that the First and Fourteenth Amendments protect the freedom to choose one's associates. . . . The selection of one's living companions involves similar choices as to the emotional, social, or economic benefits to be derived from alternative living arrangements.

*   *   *

The choice of household companions—of whether a person's 'intellectual and emotional' needs are best met by living with family, friends, professional associates or others—involves deeply personal considerations as to the kind and quality of intimate relationships within the home.

*   *   *

I would find the challenged ordinance unconstitutional. But I would not ask the village to abandon its goals of providing quiet streets, little traffic, and a pleasant and reasonably priced environment in which families might raise their children. Rather, I would commend the town to continue to pursue those purposes but by means of more carefully drawn and even-handed legislation."

Endnotes

1. 476 F.2 808 (1973).
2. 416 U.S. 1 (April 1, 1974).

Chapter Five

In the Privacy of Your Bedroom

"While I nodded, nearly napping, suddenly there came a tapping, as of someone gently rapping, rapping at my chamber door."

—Edgar Allen Poe, "The Raven"

On a hot Atlanta day in 1982, the day after Independence Day, Michael Hardwick had just finished setting up a lighting system in a gay bar. He had a beer in his hand as he left for the day. When he was about ten feet out the door and into the parking lot he remembered that the "drinking in public" law was being strictly enforced. He emptied the bottle and threw it into an empty trash can on the bar's property.

It was then that he saw an officer making a U-turn on Monroe Street. The police car pulled up to Hardwick and the officer got out of the car. He searched Hardwick, asked for identification and asked where the beer bottle was. Michael Hardwick identified himself and said that the beer bottle was in the trash can in the parking lot. The officer accused Hardwick of lying, but did not look for the bottle.

The officer, K.R. Torick, who had been harassing patrons of gay bars, issued Mr. Hardwick a complaint, much like a minor traffic ticket, for drinking in public. The complaint had two different days written at the top left corner: "Wed Thurs," and commanded Hardwick to appear in court on July 13th, 1982, or suffer a fine. July 13th, 1982 was a Tuesday.

Because he thought that his court date was on a Wednesday or a Thursday, Hardwick failed to appear in court on July 13th, 1982.

Barging and Entering

On July 13th, at 2:30 in the afternoon, Officer Torick showed up at Hardwick's house. He entered without permission, first questioning a guest, Kirk Slusser, demanding identification and requesting Hardwick's whereabouts. Slusser told the policeman that Hardwick had left earlier and would return about 5:00 p.m. Officer Torick proceeded down the apartment's hallway to the back bedroom where he barged in. He found another friend there, Bob Cheeks, and demanded identification of him. Officer Torick announced, "Tell him I will be back," as he left.

At about 4:00 that afternoon Hardwick arrived home to find his guests somewhat shaken. He then realized that he had been required to appear in court that morning. Hardwick called the courthouse and was advised to report to the clerk of the court, Jerry Coote, first thing the next morning. He was told not to worry because it takes forty-eight hours to process an arrest warrant. Michael Hardwick was concerned because Officer Torick, apparently without a warrant, had entered his home and upset his guests.

Citation given to Michael Hardwick on July 5, 1982.

Paying the Fine

Hardwick awoke early the next morning, arrived at the courthouse at 8:30, and promptly reported to the clerk. The clerk left for a few minutes and returned stating that because Hardwick had missed his court date, he had to pay the maximum fine of fifty dollars. Again he was advised not to worry because no warrant would be issued. After paying his fine, Hardwick received a receipt from the clerk as shown below:

Peeping Police

Three weeks later, on the morning of August 3rd,

Officer Torick again appeared at Hardwick's home. Torick had an arrest warrant with him concerning Hardwick's failure to appear in court on July 13th. The arrest warrant was invalid because the fine had been paid in full.

Torick entered the apartment, awakened a house guest and asked for Michael Hardwick. Mr. Slusser, the house guest, answered that he wasn't sure where Hardwick was. Officer Torick then entered Hardwick's bedroom without knocking and observed Hardwick involved in a sexual act with another man. Torick told the two men to get up and get dressed. He did not advise them of their rights.

Torick discovered a bowl with a small amount of marijuana in it and stated that both men were under arrest for sodomy and for possession of marijuana. He ordered them into his car and still did not read them their rights.

Hardwick told the officer that he had paid his fine for drinking in public and that if he would call in to verify it, or go with him to his place of employment, he would show him the receipt. Officer Torick said that he would not call in or go with Hardwick to find proof of payment because he "did not run a goddamned taxi service."

In Atlanta City Jail

Upon arriving at the Atlanta City Jail, Torick informed the processing officers that the two men were being charged with sodomy and possession of marijuana. They were placed in a holding cell with ten to twelve other men and were held for ten hours, six hours after bond was ready to be set. During incarceration some policemen taunted Hardwick and Dewitt, referring to them as "fags" and saying that they should enjoy being in the bullpen with other men. The processing officer had made a similar comment to the two men.

At 10:00 that night Hardwick and Dewitt were bonded out. Each was required to pay $275 for bond. Hardwick paid an additional fifty dollars for the earlier offense, even though he had paid this fine once already.

Sodomy in Georgia

The Georgia sodomy statute provides:

> "(a) A person commits the offense of sodomy when he performs or submits to any sexual act involving the sex organs of one person and the mouth or anus of another
> . . . .
>
> (b) A person convicted of the offense of sodomy shall be punished by imprisonment for not less than one nor more than 20 years . . . ."

The statute clearly applies to heterosexual relations as well as to homosexual relations. However, the statute is vague: it fails to define "a sexual act" and "a sexual organ." Is a female breast a sexual organ? Is kissing a sexual act? If so, a man kissing his wife's breast could be in violation of the Georgia sodomy law.

On the Offensive

The district attorney decided not to prosecute Hardwick. He stated that the state had already spent too much money on the case. A group called Georgians Opposed to Archaic Laws (GOAL) was looking for a test case to challenge the sodomy laws. When the criminal case against Michael Hardwick was dropped, GOAL asked him if he would be a plaintiff in a test case against the law.

Kathleen Wilde, a civil liberties lawyer in Atlanta, was hired to prepare the case against the sodomy law. In addition to representing Hardwick, Ms. Wilde found a married couple who was opposed to the law. In the lawsuit that she prepared, the couple, referred to as John and Mary Doe, "wished to engage in sexual activity proscribed by" the Georgia sodomy law.

On Valentine's Day in 1983, Hardwick and John and Mary Doe filed suit in the federal court in Atlanta challenging the constitutionality of the Georgia sodomy law. The suit contended that the law violated the privacy rights of citizens who desired to practice sodomy in their homes. Hardwick asserted that he was a practicing homosexual and that he was in imminent danger of arrest. The district court dismissed the case, finding that the plaintiffs had put forward no claim which entitled them to a decision in their favor.

Hardwick and the Does appealed. The court of appeals ruled in favor of Mr. Hardwick:[1]

> "The Georgia sodomy statute infringes
> upon the fundamental constitutional

rights of Michael Hardwick.

*   *   *

The Constitution prevents the States from
unduly interfering in certain individual
decisions critical to personal autonomy
because those decisions are essentially private and beyond the legitimate reach of
civilized society.

*   *   *

Hardwick desires to engage privately in
sexual activity with another consenting
adult. Although his behavior is not pro-
creative, it does not involve important as-
sociational interests."

Before the High Court

Michael J. Bowers, the Attorney General of the
State of Georgia, appealed the decision to the Supreme
Court. The Supreme Court agreed to hear the case and
set oral argument for March 31st, 1986.

Several days after the oral argument, the justices
met in conference to vote on the case. The justices
voted five to four to rule in favor of Hardwick. A few
days later, however, Justice Lewis F. Powell, Jr., of
Virginia, sent a memo to the other justices saying that
he had changed his mind. Now the vote was five to
four against Hardwick and in favor of upholding the
sodomy law. Justice Byron White wrote the majority

opinion upholding the law.[2] The court's opinion only discusses homosexual activities and completely ignores the fact that the law applies equally to heterosexual conduct.

Justice Powell cast the deciding vote and wrote a separate opinion. He said, "I cannot say the conduct condemned for hundreds of years has now become a fundamental right."

Justice Harry Blackmun took the unusual step of reading major portions of a harsh dissent from the bench on the day the decision was announced (Monday, June 30th, 1986). He said that despite "almost obsessive focus on homosexual activity" by a "bare majority" of the court, the Georgia law covers heterosexual activity as well. Blackmun said the case is not about whether there is a fundamental right to engage in homosexual acts but about "the most comprehensive of rights and the right most valued by civilized men, namely, the right to be let alone." Justice Blackmun was joined in his decision by Justices Brennan, Marshall, and Stevens.

Epilogue

Michael Hardwick was a twenty-nine-year-old bartender when he was arrested in 1982. He has moved from Atlanta to Miami, Florida, where he is studying botany and horticulture. Mr. Hardwick is a talented interior designer as well as a sculptor.

His case brought him out into the open. He learned how politics, not law, decided his case, and how the highest court of the land twisted the case into an "anti-homosexual" one.

Michael Hardwick photographed by David Vance.

Endnotes

1. 760 F.2d 1202 (1985).
2. 106 S.Ct. 2841 (1986).

PART 3
Freedom of Speech

Chapter Six

Fighting Words

"Sticks and stones will break my bones but words will never hurt me."

—Children's taunt

On Saturday afternoon, April 6th, 1940, Walter Chaplinski, twenty-six, a Jehovah's Witness, was distributing the literature of his sect on the public sidewalks of Rochester, New Hampshire, a town of about 15,000 people. Chaplinski had come with several other Jehovah's Witnesses from Shenandoah, Pennsylvania and relocated in Dover, New Hampshire, not far from Rochester. Chaplinski condemned all other religions as a racket.

Members of the local citizenry complained to the city marshall, James Bowering, Jr., that Chaplinski was denouncing all religions. Bowering told them that Chaplinski was conducting himself lawfully, and then warned Chaplinski that the crowd was getting restless.

Four school-aged children, also Jehovah's Witnesses, were carrying placards around the town square while Chaplinski continued handing out leaflets, ballyhooing his religion and denouncing other religions. He said that his leaflets contained the truth about President Roosevelt's envoy to Europe. "Religion is a racket. Read the uncensored news," he said. The city marshall stated that he had warned Chaplinski to leave the city, that Chaplinski was inciting the people, and that he had received many complaints and requests to stop him. He told Chaplinski that if a riot started Chaplinski would be responsible for it.

According to witnesses, Chaplinski made several derogatory remarks about this country. Several men brought an American flag and ordered Chaplinski to salute it. He refused to salute the flag. As a Jehovah's Witness he believed that saluting any flag is contrary to God's commandment, "Thou shalt have no other gods before me." One man asked Chaplinski to take off his glasses and he refused. The man then took them off, another man knocked Chaplinski down, and several others joined in the attack.

A Fascist and a Racketeer

Marshall Bowering had just returned to City Hall when a car drove up and notified him that there was a riot on the square. He rushed back and found Chaplinski on the ground with his papers scattered about. Bowering escorted Chaplinski to the station. While he was being escorted to the station, Chaplinski called Bowering a Fascist and a racketeer and said that the whole government of Rochester were Fascists or agents of Fascists.

Walter Chaplinski, circa 1942, courtesy of Mr. Chaplinski.

Chaplinski was charged with unlawfully using the words "Fascist" and "racketeer" under a New Hampshire law which prohibited using offensive, derisive, and annoying words and names. He was taken to the Strafford County Farm to await a hearing to be held five days later. He told Judge Gardner S. Hall that he would not furnish twenty-five dollar bail bond because he did not believe in bail.

Chaplinski was tried by Judge Hall and found guilty of the charge. He was sentenced to twelve days at the House of Corrections and was ordered to pay costs of $24.78.

He appealed to the Superior Court, but the court upheld the New Hampshire law and he was again found guilty and sentenced to serve six months at the House of Corrections. He served two weeks of the sentence before being released on bail. In March 1941, the New Hampshire Supreme Court ruled against Chaplinski, affirming his conviction. Chaplinski then filed the necessary papers with the Supreme Court of the United States, which agreed to hear his appeal.

In the United States Supreme Court

In 1942, while the United States was fighting Germany and Japan with more than fighting words, the United States Supreme Court ruled that "fighting words," which would be those words likely to cause an average person to fight, are not protected by the First Amendment.[1] Remarkably, the decision was unanimous.

Constitutional law professor Chester Antieau believes that the decision was wrong[2]:

> "'Fighting words' have been used not only by American presidents but by many other citizens, and they are a traditional aspect of our communicated freedom. Furthermore, the concept is so vague that no lawyer can adequately guide his client contemplating a public speech. Additionally, the assumption that the use of 'fighting words' generally leads to breaches of the peace must be seriously questioned. Even if fisticuffs follow at times, the interests of society can better be served by chastising the violent and not the verbal."

If we allow police to arrest speakers because of the content of their speeches then the First Amendment is meaningless. "Fighting words" to one person are dinner table conversation to another. Because of this it is impossible to define them, and the average person has no idea of where free speech stops and fighting words begin.

Epilogue

Even in the 1980s, the Supreme Court often refers to the *Chaplinsky* case as an exception to free speech. Because of this the fighting words exception lives on.

Recently at his home in St. Petersburg, Florida, Walter Chaplinski stated that the case enriched his life. He stated that his imprisonment for eight months taught him about justice in this country, and that he experienced religious persecution that Christians experienced a thousand years ago. After the Supreme Court's ruling he worked as a special pioneer Witness, spreading the gospel for the Jehovah's Witnesses.

Mr. Chaplinski is now seventy-six years old and is retired. He worked as a stone mason for twenty-seven years. He and his wife of thirty-eight years moved to Florida in 1960.

Endnotes

1. 315 U.S. 568 (1942). The Supreme Court misspelled Mr. Chaplinski's name.

2. *Modern Constitutional Law*, New York: Lawyers Co-operative Publishing Co., 1969, p. 23.

Chapter Seven

Dirty Words

"I could never succeed in 'defining it' intelligibly," but *"I know it when I see it."*

—Justice Potter Stewart on pornography

"Pornography is whatever gives a judge an erection."

—Anonymous lawyer

In 1962, Ralph Ginzburg published sexually oriented magazines and books, including *Eros, Liaison* and *The Housewife's Handbook on Selective Promiscuity. Eros* was a hard-cover magazine, *The Housewife's Handbook* a short book and *Liaison* a bi-weekly newsletter.

Eros

Eros contained a wide variety of articles, including

"The Short Story" by Ray Bradbury, "President Harding's Second Lady," "Was Shakespeare a Homosexual?," "Memoirs of a Male Chaperone," "Bawdy Limericks," "The Sexual Side of Anti-Semitism," "Natural Superiority of Women as Eroticists," "Sex and the Bible," "Lysistrata," and six other articles. A photoessay was included, entitled "Black and White in Color," which portrayed a black man and a white woman in the nude.

Eros also included a lengthy excerpt from *My Life and Loves,* by Frank Harris. *Eros* was a hard-cover magazine which cost twenty-five dollars per year. This work received extensive literary commentary in other publications, including *The New Yorker, New York Review of Books, Library Journal, Newsweek, New York Times Book Review* and *New Republic. Eros* won numerous awards including the prestigious award from the Society of Publication Designers and a Gold Medal from the Art Directors Club of New York.

Liaison

Liaison was a newsletter. Volume One, Issue One included articles entitled "Slaying the Sex Dragon," "Semen in the Diet" and "Sing a Song of Sex Life." This issue also included digests of two articles concerning sex and sexual relations which had earlier appeared in professional journals and a report of an interview with a psychotherapist.

The Housewife's Handbook on Selective Promiscuity

The *Handbook* is a sexual autobiography of Rey

Anthony (Mrs. Lillian Maxine Serett) detailing the author's sexual experiences from age three to age thirty-six. The book include's the author's views on sex education, laws regulating private consentual adult sexual practices and the equality of women in sexual relationships. Before selling the rights of her book to Mr. Ginzburg, the author printed it privately. She sold some 12,000 copies of the book to medical and psychiatric professionals.

Advertising

The *Handbook* was advertised by mail. The advertisement included most of the introduction of the book, written by Dr. Albert Ellis. Dr. Ellis considered the book to be informational and to have therapeutic value. His introduction included a description of the book's sexual imagery. The advertisement included a guarantee that if the book was censored by the post office, a full refund would be made.

One *Eros* advertisement claimed:

> "*Eros* is a child of its times . . . . It is the result of recent court decisions that have realistically interpreted America's obscenity laws and that have given to this a country a new breadth of freedom of expression . . . . *Eros* takes advantage of this new freedom of expression. It is *the* magazine of sexual candor."

A mailing piece promoting *Liaison* appealed to its readers: "Though *Liaison* handles the subjects of love

and sex with complete candor, I wish to
make it clear that it is not a scandal
sheet and it is not written for the man in
the street. *Liaison* is aimed at intelligent,
educated adults who can accept love and
sex as a part of life."

The Statute

Congress passed the federal obscenity statute in 1865.
This law declares that "obscene, lewd, lascivious,
indecent, filthy or vile matter and devices" (and advertisements for them) are "nonmailable matter." This federal law punishes persons who attempt to mail or actually mail "nonmailable matter" by a fine of up to
$5,000 and/or imprisonment of up to five years.

The Grand Jury and the Grand Judge

On March 15th, 1963, the Grand Jury sitting in Philadelphia returned a twenty-eight count indictment
charging that Ralph Ginzburg and his corporations violated the federal obscenity law. The case was assigned
to Judge Body. Mr. Ginzburg wanted the case disposed
of quickly so that he could continue publishing his
books and magazines without the charges pending. His
attorneys filed a motion to dismiss the charges, but the
court denied the motion. Ginzburg made the fatal mistake of waiving his right to a jury trial and submitted
to a trial before the judge.

The trial took five days. Experts were called to
show the value of the publications in question. The

author of the *Handbook* was called as a witness. The chairman of the Fine Arts Department of New York University testified that the photographs were outstanding, beautiful and artistic.

The judge found that only four of the fifteen articles in *Eros* were obscene. He found, however, that "*Eros* has no saving grace. The items of possible merit might be considered innocuous and a mere guise to avoid the law and in large measure enhance the pruriency of the entire work."

The court disregarded testimony concerning the value of the *Handbook* to sexual therapists. Judge Body said, "Any testimony to this effect is expressly disbelieved."

The judge similarly found that *Liaison* included "jokes and rhymes which clearly go beyond contemporary community standards of humor, even in applying liberal nightclub standards."

Judge Body found all three publications to be obscene and sentenced Ralph Ginzburg to five years in federal prison.

The Appeals

The federal court of appeals affirmed the lower court's ruling. Ginzburg's lawyers sought review in the United States Supreme Court and the highest court agreed to hear the case.

In 1957, the Supreme Court had decided that obscene literature was not protected by the First Amendment.[1] Justice William Brennan wrote the *Roth* opinion, which stated that books and magazines were obscene when, to the average person, applying contemporary community standards, the dominant theme of the material, taken as a whole, appeals to prurient interest. In a later opinion, the court added that the material could not be obscene unless it "was utterly without redeeming social value."[2]

Relying on this earlier decision, Justice Brennan wrote the opinion for the court in the *Ginzburg* case. He found that the "leer of the sensualist" permeated the advertising for the three publications and cited the advertisements quoted above. He remarked that Dr. Ellis is heavily quoted in one brochure but that the solicitation was "indiscriminate" because it was not limited to physicians or psychiatrists.

The Supreme Court ruled that because Ginzburg "pandered" (appealed to the sexual interests of the readers), the material in question would be considered obscene, even though the same materials would not be considered obscene if sold to a sex therapist. Brennan stated that Ginzburg and his companies

> "did not sell the book to such a limited audience, or focus . . . on its supposed therapeutic or educational value; rather they deliberately emphasized the sexually provocative aspects of the work, in order to catch the salaciously disposed."

The vote of the court was five to four. Justice Hugo Black, in dissent, wrote that Ginzburg was condemned

by the court to serve five years in prison for distributing printed matter about sex, an offense which no
one could possibly have known to be criminal. He
stated that he was opposed to government censorship of
any kind, since the First Amendment forbids it.

Justice William O. Douglas also dissented:

> "The advertisements of our best maga-
> zines are chock-full of thighs, ankles,
> calfs, bosoms, eyes and hair, to draw the
> potential buyer's attention to lotions,
> tires, food, liquor, clothing, autos, and
> even insurance policies. The sexy adver-
> tisement neither adds to nor detracts
> from the quality of the merchandise be-
> ing offered for sale. And I do not see
> how it adds to or detracts one whit from
> the legality of the book being distributed.
> A book should stand on its own, irre-
> spective of the reasons why it was writ-
> ten or the wiles used in selling it."

Justice Douglas also said that

> "*Liaison's* appeal is to the ribald sense of
> humor which is—for better or worse—a
> part of our culture. A mature society
> would not suppress this newsletter as ob-
> scene but would simply ignore it."

Douglas concluded:

> "I think that this is the ideal of the Free
> Society written into our Constitution. We

have no business acting as censors or endowing any group with censorship powers. It is shocking to me for us to send to prison anyone for publishing anything, especially tracts so distant from any incitement to action as the ones before us."

Justices John Harlan and Potter Stewart also wrote separate dissenting opinions. Justice Stewart, who is quoted at the beginning of this chapter, wrote a brilliant dissent:

"There was testimony at his trial that these publications possess artistic and social merit. Personally, I have a hard time discerning any. Most of the material strikes me as both vulgar and unedifying. But if the First Amendment means anything, it means that a man cannot be sent to prison merely for distributing publications which offend a judge's aesthetic sensibilities, mine or any other's.

Censorship reflects a society's lack of confidence in itself. It is a hallmark of an authoritarian regime. Long ago those who wrote our First Amendment charted a different course. They believed a society can be truly strong only when it is truly free."

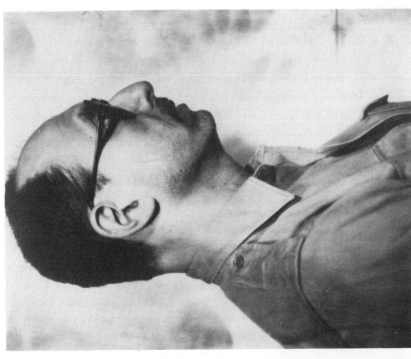

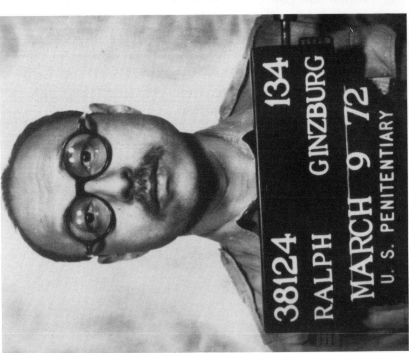

Publisher Ralph Ginzburg (prisoner number 38124) photographed on his admission to U.S. Penitentiary on March 9, 1972, courtesy of Mr. Ginzburg.

Epilogue

Years after the decision was handed down Justice Stewart remarked at Columbia University that the two worst Supreme Court decisions were the *Dred Scott* and *Ginzburg* decisions. Justice Brennan, who authored the *Ginzburg* decision, has changed his mind, and now believes that *Roth* and *Ginzburg* and a slew of other obscenity decisions were mistakes.[3] In the intervening years, however, the composition of the court has grown more conservative and Justice Brennan finds himself in the liberal minority.

Censorship is alive and well in the United States. The Federal Communications Commission has recently warned radio stations to avoid obscenities, threatening to challenge license renewals. It is necessary for Congress to repeal the federal obscenities statute and to direct that the FCC and other government agencies abandon their attempts to serve as national censors.

Ralph Ginzburg served eight months at Allenwood Federal Prison Camp in Pennsylvania. He was fined $42,000 and paid his lawyers nearly a quarter of a million dollars. Ginzburg is now the successful publisher of *Moneysworth*, *American Business*, and *Better Living*. He feels that his trial, conviction and appeal ruined his career and deprived society of the first and only psychology magazine concerned with sex.

Endnotes

1. *Roth v. United States*, 354 U.S. 476.
2. *Memoirs v. Massachusetts*, 383 U.S. 413.
3. *Paris Adult Theatre I v. Slaton*, 413 U.S. 49 (1973).

Chapter Eight

Unpopular Speakers

"I disapprove of what you say, but I will defend to the death your right to say it."

—Voltaire

Syracuse city officials granted a permit for O. John Rogge, a former U.S. assistant attorney general, to speak at a public school building on March 8, 1949, on the subject of racial discrimination and civil liberties. He was coming to coming to Syracuse to talk about a New Jersey case in which three blacks had been sentenced to the electric chair for killing a storekeeper. Rogge and others believed that the sentences were unjust.

On the day that the speech was to be given, authorities cancelled the permit. The Young Progressives, sponsors of the speech, arranged for Mr. Rogge to speak at the Hotel Syracuse instead of the public school.

Irving Feiner at Syracuse University in 1949, courtesy of Mr. Feiner.

Irving Feiner

Irving Feiner was a member of the Young Progressives. Feiner, who grew up in the Bronx, was the son of an immigrant Polish Jew. Once, while riding a train from New York to the South, he saw a black family behind a set of curtains in a segregated dining car. They were roped off from everyone else, and Feiner said, "I'll never forget that. It made a tremendous impression on me." It was experiences like this one that made Feiner, while a student at Syracuse University, join the Young Progressives, a group that advocated equal rights for Negroes, a precursor of the civil rights movement. Feiner entered the university in 1947 on the GI Bill, after serving in the Army during World War II.

To publicize the new meeting place, Feiner stood on a wooden box on the sidewalk near the hotel and addressed a group of people. Feiner was speaking into a microphone, which was attached to speakers on an automobile parked on McBride Street. Between five and ten other Young Progressives were distributing leaflets to the crowd and helping with the sound system. Feiner began to spread the news about the last minute change, informing the crowd that city officials were responsible. In the course of his remarks, he called Syracuse Mayor Costello a "champagne-sipping bum." He also called President Truman a "bum" and compared the American Legion to Nazi Gestapo agents.

A Gathering Crowd

A complaint concerning the gathering was made by telephone to the police department, and at about 6:30 p.m. two officers, Flynn and Cook, were dispatched to the scene to investigate.

As Officer Cook approached the scene in his police car, he had to slow down and almost stop because the crowd was bulging into the street. Officer Flynn, an acting sergeant, arrived in a police car a few minutes

later and found that Officer Cook had already arrived.
They noted that a crowd of seventy-five or eighty
people, both black and white, had gathered around Feiner.

Some of the crowd spread out into the street.
Pedestrians trying to use the sidewalk had to walk in
the street to get around the crowd. As the officers attempted to maintain the crowd on the sidewalk, Officer
Flynn thought he heard "angry muttering." He had
trouble getting through the crowd and felt that people
were getting "restless."

As Feiner continued, Flynn believed he saw some
pushing and shoving. "Some were calm and some were
not—they were discussing the speech, pro and con."
There was no disorder, however, as Officer Flynn
testified, so after telephoning the police station from a
nearby store, Flynn and Cook returned to the scene to
mingle with the crowd and observe.

Feiner began to appeal to the black people, in particular. He said that in current society, Negroes did not
have equal rights. He wanted the crowd to "rise up
and fight for their rights and go arm in arm, black and
white alike, to the Hotel Syracuse to hear John Rogge."
Although this appeal seems to suggest that blacks and
whites unite, Officer Flynn got the impression that Feiner was trying to arouse the blacks against the whites.
He noted that people were stirred by the remarks.

The Threat of Violence

Then, a man approached the officers and said, "If
you don't get that son-of-a-bitch off, I will go over and
get him off there myself." This was the only threat of

violence that Flynn had heard up to that point, but he testified that some other people did comment that the police force seemed unable to handle the situation, and, that "they did not see why they had to put up with that kind of stuff in the neighborhood."

At this point, Officer Flynn figured that Feiner's speech had gone far enough. In his opinion, the crowd was getting to the point where they might become unruly. True, there was no actual disturbance, but Flynn claimed that "we stepped in to prevent it from resulting in a fight." He approached Irving Feiner, not to arrest him, but to get him to break up the congregation. Flynn asked Feiner to get off the box, but Feiner kept on talking. Officer Flynn waited a minute, then demanded that he get down, but Feiner refused. Neither Flynn nor officer Cook tried to do anything to the man who made the threat against Feiner. While Flynn was talking to Feiner the crowd was quiet.

Flynn told Feiner that he was under arrest and reached up to take hold of him. Feiner stepped down off the box and announced into the microphone that "the law has arrived, and I suppose they will take over now." He was then arrested and told that he was being charged with "unlawful assembly." Later, because the officers believed there was not enough evidence to convict Feiner of this charge, they changed it to "disorderly conduct."

But the new charge seems no more compelling. Feiner had a legal right to give his speech and had the right to use loud-speaking equipment. The law for disorderly conduct requires citizens to obey "reasonable police orders." Police often use disorderly conduct charges as a catch-all charge when they cannot find another law that applies to someone's "offending" conduct. A police order to "be quiet" when someone is interfering with an arrest is one thing; an order when a public speaker is addressing a crowd is quite different. However the "disorderly conduct" offense can be applied in both situations.

The Conviction

In May of that year, the case was tried before Judge William Bamerick in the special sessions court, and Irving Feiner was found guilty and sentenced to thirty days in the county jail. He served five days before being released on bail, because he had decided to appeal the case.

The American Civil Liberties Union supported Feiner's appeal, after the county court, and then the New York Court of Appeals, the state's highest court, affirmed Feiner's conviction.

Meanwhile, Feiner was expelled from Syracuse University, because he had been convicted of disorderly conduct, upending his plans to go to law school. Two law schools that had accepted him withdrew their approvals, as he had not received his undergraduate degree.

At the Nation's Highest Tribunal

In the McCarthy days of 1951, Feiner's case made its way the United States Supreme Court where its decision was handed down on Monday, January 15th. The Supreme Court, in a six to three decision, ruled that Feiner was legally arrested, because he passed the bounds of argument or persuasion and undertook "incitement to riot." Chief Justice Vinson wrote:

> "We are well aware that the ordinary murmuring and objections of a hostile audience cannot be allowed to silence a speaker, and are also mindful of the possible danger of giving overzealous police officials complete discretion to break up otherwise lawful public meetings."[1]

Justice Vinson gave lip service to free speech, while giving the local gendarmes complete discretion to stop unpopular speakers. The crowd was not violent and did no more than mutter. The threat to the peace came from one person in the crowd, not from the speaker.

Justice Black wrote a blistering dissent:

> "I think this conviction makes a mockery out of Free Speech guarantees of the First and Fourteenth Amendments. The end result of the affirmance here is to approve a simple and readily available technique by which cities and states can with impunity subject all speeches, political or otherwise, on streets or

elsewhere, to the supervision and censorship of the local police. I will have no part or parcel in this holding which I view as a long step toward totalitarian authority.

*   *   *

I reject the implication of the Court's opinion that the police had no obligation to protect petitioner's constitutional right to talk. The police of course have power to prevent breaches of the peace. But if, in the name of preserving order, they ever can interfere with a lawful public speaker, they must first make all reasonable efforts to protect him. Here the policemen did not even pretend to protect petitioner."

Justices Douglas and Minton also dissented.

Epilogue

While his case was pending, Feiner went back to New York and found a job in the printing business. In February, Irving Feiner came back to Onondaga County and served the remaining twenty-five days of his sentence at the Jamesville Penitentiary. He then went back to his job in New York, started his own print shop, got married and moved to the suburbs, where he raised two daughters.

He later set up "Fish, Fish, Fish" in Nyack, New

York where he sells exotic and rare tropical fish. But because of his Supreme Court case, he never became a lawyer.

Thirty-five years after being expelled from Syracuse University, Feiner was readmitted under a special program to complete his college degree. He completed the credits he was lacking when expelled, and in 1984 was awarded his Bachelor of Arts degree. Although Feiner never did make it to law school, he occasionally lectures to constitutional law students on his case.

Endnotes

1. 340 U.S. 315 (1951).

Chapter Nine

Going Door-to-Door

"Behold, I stand at the door and knock."

—Revelation 3:20

Knocking on doors to support political causes or to sell Girl Scout cookies or wares has been an American institution since before the Constitution was enacted. This chapter includes two cases which severely undercut the right to go door-to-door for commercial or political reasons.

The Postal Monopoly

Did you know that despite the fact that you pay for your own mailbox, the government regulates what can be put into it? Have you ever put a note in your neighbor's mailbox without putting a postage stamp on it? If so, then you, like most Americans, have broken a federal law.

In May, 1976, in New York state, volunteers for the Hilltop Farms Civic Association (part of the Saw Mill Valley Civic Association) hand-delivered notices to the homes in their area. The notice told of a town meeting to be held on June 3rd. As usual, the notices were put in mailboxes, and no postage was put on them. The civic association did not have much money, so it relied on volunteer labor rather than the U.S. Post Office to deliver its notices.

About the same time, political materials for Jimmy Carter, Walter Mondale, Senator Patrick Moynihan, Congressman J. Edward Meyer and various candidates for state offices were put into mailboxes in the same manner.

Then, on June 2, 1976, Walter Rostenberg, the postmaster for White Plains, New York, learned that the notices were being put into mailboxes without postage. He wrote a letter to the leader of the civic association, enclosing a copy of the postal regulations. Rostenberg warned that the practice was illegal and that failure to comply with the law would result in a fine of up to $300.

In 1934, Congress passed a law which provided:

> "Whoever knowingly and willfully deposits any mailable matter such as statements of accounts, circulars, sale bills, or other like matter, on which no postage has been paid, in any letter box established, approved, or accepted by the Postal Service for the receipt or delivery of mail matter on any mail route with intent to avoid payment of lawful postage

thereon, shall for each offense be fined
no more than $300."[1]

In February, 1977, the Saw Mill Valley Civic Association, with other civic organizations, filed suit seeking
relief from the Postal Service's threatened enforcement
of the 1934 law. The plaintiffs argued that enforcement
of the law would inhibit their ability to communicate
with residents in their towns and would, thus, deny
them freedom of speech and press, secured by the First
Amendment.

The case was assigned to federal Judge William
Connor. Attorneys for the Post Office moved to have
the case dismissed without trial, because they contended
that the statute was constitutional. Judge Connor granted the government's motion and dismissed the case. He
ruled:

> "[T]he Constitution does not guarantee
> plaintiffs an absolute right to the most
> efficient or effective means of communi-
> cation."[2]

The civic associations appealed Judge Connor's
ruling. The three judge panel of the Second Circuit
Court of Appeals in New York City agreed with the
citizens groups. They ruled that the case should not
have been dismissed without a trial. Quoting an earlier
Supreme Court case, Judge Irving Kaufman wrote:

> "Freedom of press 'necessarily embraces
> pamphlets and leaflets. These indeed have
> been historic weapons in the defense of
> liberty, as the pamphlets of Thomas
> Paine and others in our history abundant-

ly attest.' And probably the most effective way of ensuring that such literature reaches its intended audience is house-to-house distribution.

*   *   *

Moreover, the individual householder's right to receive information cannot be ignored."[3]

The Court of Appeals reversed the dismissal and sent the case back to Judge Connor, of the district court, for a trial. At the trial, the Post Office introduced evidence that the purpose of the statute was to protect mail revenues and to prevent overcrowding of mailboxes. The citizens group argued that they could not afford to pay for postage and, furthermore, that the Post Office was slow and that its volunteers delivered notices much more quickly. The district court found the Postal Service's reasons to be insufficient and ruled that the statute was unconstitutional:

> "Plaintiffs have shown that the burden on their ability to communicate ideas, positions on local issues and civic information to their constituents is substantial.
>
> *   *   *
>
> The court concludes that the cost to free expression of imposing this burden outweighs the showing made by the Postal Service of its need to enforce the statute to promote effective delivery and protection of the mails."[4]

Before the U.S. Supreme Court

The Post Office appealed the lower court's ruling directly to the U.S. Supreme Court. This is allowed when a court rules that a federal statute is unconstitutional. The court reversed Judge Connor's decision by a seven to two vote. Only Justices Marshall and Stevens dissented.

Justice Marshall wrote that "door to door distribution of circulars is essential to the poorly financed causes of little people."[5]

Justice Stevens wrote a thoughtful dissent:

> "The mailbox is private property. If a private party—by using volunteer workers or by operating more efficiently—can deliver written communications for less than the cost of postage, then public interest would be well served by transferring that portion of the mail delivery business out of the public domain. I see no reason to prohibit competition simply to prevent reduction in the size of a subsidized monopoly.

> *   *   *

> I have the impression that the general public is at best only dimly aware of the law and that numerous otherwise law-abiding citizens regularly violate it with impunity."

Epilogue

Congress should amend the Postal law to allow non-profit organizations and individuals to put notices and leaflets in mailboxes. When the law makes criminals of us all, we lose respect for it. Since many of us leave notes for neighbors or leave flyers for political candidates or for the Red Cross or Girl Scouts in mailboxes, and still more of us indirectly endorse such actions by responding to flyers others leave, we are all federal criminals.

Selling Magazines Door-to-Door

Jack Breard was a regional representative, based in Dallas, Texas, for the Keystone Readers Service, a company that sold magazine subscriptions by door-to-door solicitations. The magazines they sold included the *Saturday Evening Post, Ladies' Home Journal, Country Gentleman, Holiday, Newsweek, American Home, Cosmopolitan, Esquire, Parents, Today's Woman* and *True* magazines. At the time, the early 1950s, annual subscriptions to these magazines were about two dollars.

Breard would send a team of solicitors, often college students, to canvass a town for a few days and then move on to another town. They would stay in inexpensive hotels, with two or three salesman to a room. Pay was on a commission basis.

Jack Breard photographed in 1950s, courtesy Jack Breard, Jr.

Green River Ordinances

Green River Ordinances got their name from the town of Green River, Wyoming, where they originated. These ordinances prohibited the practice of selling anything door-to-door, except dairy or grocery products, unless the homeowner or resident of the property requested the item. Dairy and grocery products were excluded because in the early 1950s, when most Green River Ordinances were passed, it was common practice to sell these items door-to-door, and it was convenient for the consumer. But all other solicitation—even by Girl Scouts, Little Leaguers or Red Cross volunteers, whether they be selling cookies, candles or magazines—was strictly prohibited.

Alexandria, Louisiana was one of over 400 towns and cities to pass a Green River Ordinance. Their ordinance declared violations to be a misdemeanor and provided for a fine of twenty-five dollars or a sentence of thirty days in jail.

On June 28, 1949, Jack Breard and his crew were working on the streets of Alexandria, Louisiana when he was arrested for violating the law, regarding door-to-door solicitation.

In the Halls of Justice

Gus Voltz was the judge assigned to hear Mr. Breard's case in the City Court of Alexandria, Parish of Rapides. Attorneys for Breard argued that the First Amendment right of free speech and press allowed him to solicit subscriptions for magazines by knocking on doors. They argued that the magazines certainly enjoyed protection under the amendment, and that more than half of the subscribers to magazines at that time were signed up by neighborhood solicitors.

Jack Breard was tried for his offense before Judge Voltz without a jury. Judge Voltz found him guilty and imposed a fine of twenty-five dollars or thirty days in jail. Breard posted an appeal bond of a hundred dollars.

Mr. Breard's case came before Louisiana's highest court within one year. The courts of Louisiana were not sympathetic to out-of-towner Breard and his band of young solicitors. The Louisiana Supreme Court, while affirming Jack Breard's conviction, stated:

> "A man's home is his castle. No one has any vested prerogative to invade another's privacy. Each community knows its own problems best."[6]

The United States Supreme Court

The Supreme Court agreed to hear Mr. Breard's case and set oral argument for March, 1951. Breard's attorneys were optimistic because eight years earlier the court had ruled that cities and states could not enforce laws which taxed door-to-door sales of religious literature.

On June 4, 1951, by a vote of six to three, the court issued its decision.[7] The court ruled that the ordinance was valid and that it did not impose any improper restraint on free speech or on freedom of the press.

The court held that because the solicitations were for
profit, they could be prohibited. The opinion distinguished between free distributions and commercial solicitations. The court still affirmed the right to go
door-to-door to hand out free publications.

Chief Justice Vinson, who rarely dissents, and who
wrote the majority opinion for the court in the *Feiner*
case, which was decided just five months earlier (see
previous chapter), wrote a strong dissenting opinion.
Joining the Chief Justice in dissent were Justices Hugo
Black and William O. Douglas. In Justice Vinson's
opinion, the Alexandria ordinance was a regulation of
interstate commerce, which was a function of Congress,
not of local city councils.

Justice Black wrote a separate dissent, resting on the
First Amendment:

> "The constitutional sanctuary for the
> press must necessarily include liberty to
> publish and to circulate. In view of our
> economic system, it must also include
> freedom to solicit paying subscribers. Of
> course homeowners can if they wish for-
> bid newsboys, reporters or magazine so-
> licitors to ring their doorbells. But when
> the homeowner himself has not done this,
> I believe that the First Amendment,
> interpreted with due regard for the
> freedoms it guarantees, bars laws like the
> present ordinance which punish persons
> who peacefully go from door to door as
> agents of the press."

Epilogue

Jack Breard's case did not cause the end of the *Saturday Evening Post* or *Ladies' Home Journal*, or make it impossible for customers to renew their subscriptions. But because of the decision, many college students lost a source of income, and magazine publishers had to look for other ways to sell subscriptions.

Jack Breard died in 1959 at the age of 49. Magazine subscriptions are now sold by television advertising and by direct mail. Jack Breard, Jr. has adopted his father's career and sells magazine subscriptions. He said that magazines are still sold door-to-door, but not like they were in the 1940s.

Conclusions

While each of these two cases, on its own, might be considered minor, each represents a significant deterioration of our right to free speech. Cities and states have the power to prohibit the door-to-door solicitation of businesses. The Post Office and Congress have put up a barrier to the use of mailboxes. In the next chapter, another mode of communication is eliminated; the handing out of leaflets in shopping malls. If citizens cannot reach people at their homes and cannot reach them where they shop, what First Amendment freedoms are left?

Concerning the concept that "a man's home is his

castle," the Supreme Court uses this argument only when a minor intrusion is made into the home by private citizens. See chapter twenty on how the court deals with government intrusion into the home.

Of course, some citizens do not want to be bothered by having people knock on their doors or by having leaflets left in their mailboxes. These people have the right to put out a small sign saying either "No solicitors" or "U.S. mail only." I believe that a law protecting the right of citizens to limit receipt of messages would be constitutional. Citizens have a right to be let alone, as well as to receive information. But unless a citizen asserts his right to be let alone, the right of others to communicate their ideas should prevail.

Endnotes

1. 18 U.S.C. Section 1725.

2. 448 F. Supp. 159 (March 29, 1978).

3. 586 F. 2d 935 (October 30, 1978).

4. 490 F. Supp. 157 (April 24, 1980).

5. 453 U.S. 114 (June 21, 1981), quoting *Martin v. City of Struthers*, 319 U.S. 141, 146.

6. 47 So 2nd 553, 556 (June 30, 1950).

7. 341 U.S. 622 (1951).

Chapter Ten

The Malling of America

"We've got it all at Springfield Mall."

—Advertising slogan

In November of 1968, a week after Richard Nixon won the November 5th election, Lyndon Baines Johnson was still President of the United States, and the Vietnam War and the protest movement were both being waged at full tilt. More than 500,000 American soldiers were in Vietnam at the time.

On Thursday, November 14, 1968, Donald Tanner, Susan Roberts, Betsy Wheeler and one or two others handed out leaflets inviting the public to a meeting to protest the draft and the Vietnam War. The leafleteers were members of "The Resistance Community," and their handouts invited people to talks about the draft board, a potluck dinner, a communion and a dance at Reed College. Copies of the actual leaflets handed out that day are reproduced on the next two pages.

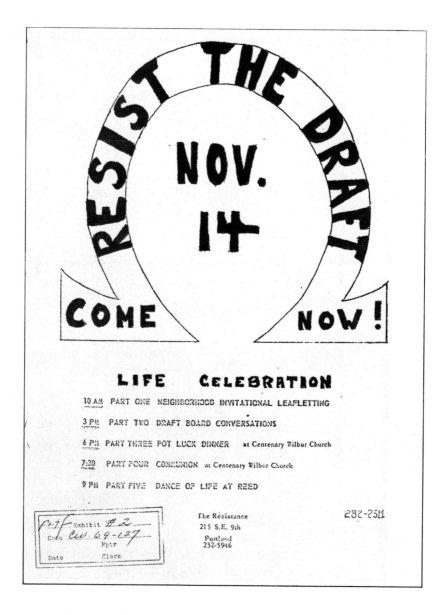

Leaflet handed out by Resistance Community at Lloyd Center Mall.

The RESISTANCE COMMUNITY cordially invites you to a CELEBRATION of LIFE

The brothers & sisters of the community will be affirming their commitment to Life by severing their connection with the Selective Service System and the international murder that it supports.

A COMMUNAL FEAST AND LITURGY OF LIBERATION WILL BEGIN AT 6:00PM AT CENTENARY WILBUR CHURCH TO BE FOLLOWED BY A RECEPTION WITH MUSIC AND DANCE AT REED COLLEGE.

We cannot resurrect the dead; however, we can prevent the living from joining them. Come join us as we celebrate the end of the old and the beginning of the new— OurLife together as Brothers-in-Love.

Invitation to Celebration of Life handed out at Lloyd Center Mall.

They distributed their leaflets at the Lloyd Center
Mall in Portland, Oregon, in a peaceful manner. The
leafleteers were scattered in different sections of the
large shopping mall. They were quiet and orderly; only
one citizen complained about their activities.

Tanner, Roberts and Wheeler were approached by
security guards who were wearing uniforms virtually
identical to those worn by the Portland police. The
security guards were armed and had the power to
arrest citizens.

The guards said that the leafleteers would be arrested for trespassing, if they persisted in their activities.
Donald Tanner told one of the security officers that he
wanted to talk to the people in charge concerning the
policy of the mall which prohibited citizens from handing out information. He was taken to see security
guard Captain Clifford P. Boss. Captain Boss stated that
if Tanner refused to leave Lloyd Center, he would be
arrested for trespassing. Because of the threat of arrest,
the leafleteers left the mall.

The Mall at Lloyd Center

Lloyd Center Mall is privately owned and is located
within the city limits of Portland, Oregon. The city
closed several streets and gave the streets to the devel-
opers, so that an urban mall could be built to compete
with suburban stores.

Lloyd Mall is like many other enclosed malls in the
United States with covered climate-controlled pedestrian
walkways connecting some sixty retail stores. The mall,
which is open to the public twenty-four hours a day,

includes twenty-five acres of stores and twenty acres of parking.

The mall is like the city streets that it replaced: on every Veterans' Day, a parade with flags, drummers and color guard units takes place, and a speech is given on the valor of American soldiers. During the 1968 presidential campaign, candidates Eugene McCarthy, Robert Kennedy and Richard Nixon gave speeches at the mall at Lloyd Center. The auditorium at the mall was used to provide television coverage of the 1964 Oregon presidential primary election.

Several politicians and organizations have been denied use of the mall at Lloyd Center. Oregon Governor Tom McCall was denied an opportunity to make a speech there. The March of Dimes and Hadassah, a Jewish organization, were also denied use of the mall.

The Salvation Army has been permitted to use the mall to raise funds during the Christmas season. The American Legion is permitted to sell "Buddy Poppies," and the Boy Scouts have been allowed to set up displays there. The mall maintains a public information center where pamphlets on the Portland Zoo, the Sanctuary of Our Sorrowful Mother and other topics are available. The Mall has also displayed National Guard weaponry and equipment, and, because of this, some people referred to the mall as "Fort Lloyd."

Malls Across America

In 1968, shopping malls were just starting to sprout up around the country. By 1987, enclosed shopping malls dominated the retail market in the United States. There are now 25,000 covered shopping malls in the U.S. They have become our town squares. Shopping malls ring up more than fifty-two percent of the nation's retail sales, excluding sales of automotive products, a total of more than $300 billion dollars every year.

In Federal Court in Oregon

Donald Tanner, Susan Roberts and Betsy Wheeler felt that they had a right to hand out leaflets in the mall. The mall was open to the public and *everyone* went to the Lloyd Center Mall to shop. Leafletting at the mall was the only effective way to reach many people. Handing out flyers was an American tradition since Thomas Paine handed out *Common Sense* more than 200 years ago.

After being threatened with arrest, they left the mall and consulted with Attorney Carl Neil. Mr. Neil advised them that the First Amendment gave them a right to hand out leaflets at shopping malls. He advised them that the *Logan Valley case* had just been decided by the Supreme Court, giving workers the right to picket at a privately owned shopping mall.[1] The Supreme Court's ruling in that case appeared to extend First Amendment protections to private shopping areas.

Neil studied the laws that allowed the Lloyd Corporation to take over city streets and filed a detailed lawsuit against the mall owners in March of 1969. The case was assigned to Chief Judge Gus J. Solomon. After hearing evidence in the case, Judge Solomon ruled that the Resistance Community, and other groups, had the right to hand out leaflets at the mall and enjoined the Lloyd Corporation from interfering with people handing out leaflets. He ruled that the mall was the "functional equivalent of a public business district."[2]

The Appeals

The Lloyd Corporation filed an appeal to the Ninth Circuit Court of Appeals. The appeal was heard by a panel of three judges who, ruling unanimously, upheld the decision of Judge Solomon.[3].

The owners of the mall then sought review in the Supreme Court, which the court granted. The nation's highest court heard arguments on April 18, 1972, and issued its opinion on June 22nd of that year.

By the closest of margins, the Supreme Court overturned the rulings of the lower courts and ruled that there is no First Amendment right to hand out leaflets at privately owned shopping malls.[4] The court, which had ruled four years earlier that unions had the right to picket in private shopping malls, decided to limit its earlier ruling. In 1946, the court had ruled that people living in a company-owned town in Alabama had the right to free speech in the streets of that town.[5] The court's ruling in *Lloyd v. Tanner* significantly undercuts the court's earlier rulings regarding the exercise of the right to free speech in malls and towns owned by private corporations.

Four justices vigorously dissented. Justice Marshall, joined by Justices Douglas, Brennan and Stewart, wrote:

> "In sum, the Lloyd Center is an integral part of the Portland Community. From its inception, the city viewed it as a 'business district' of the city and depended on it to supply much-needed employment opportunities. To insure the success of the Center, the city carefully integrated it into the pattern of streets already established and planned future development of the streets around the Center. It is plain, therefore, that Lloyd Center is the equivalent of a public 'business district' . . . .

*   *   *

> When there are no effective means of communication, free speech is a mere shibboleth. I believe that the First Amendment requires it to be a reality."

Epilogue

In the fifteen years that have passed since *Lloyd v. Tanner* was announced by the court, our country has become more suburban and more mall oriented. Enclosed shopping malls have truly become the town centers of the 1980s. Political candidates often use malls to leaflet and campaign, but do so solely at the discretion of the mall owners, whose decisions can be based upon their personal biases and prejudices, which are unrelated to the public's right to received information.

The Supreme Court's decision was based on the rights of property owners. However, when enclosed malls invite the public to shop, they are waiving their rights to completely regulate their own property. The court has recognized that store owners cannot exclude patrons because of their race, sex or religion. Similarly, the mall owners should not be able to restrict peaceful leafletting in the common areas of shopping malls. If a shopping mall security guard overhears a person talking politics, the guard has no right to evict the speaker. Similarly, the guard should have no right to eject someone for handing a written statement to another shopper.

The Framers of the Constitution did not intend so great a role for store owners in regulating free speech. They certainly did not envision corporate-owned enclosed shopping malls. If we are truly a democracy, then we must return the right of free speech to our shopping districts, either by a new Supreme Court ruling, by legislative action at the state and local level, or by a constitutional amendment.

So far, the highest court in three states (California, Washington and Connecticut) have ruled that citizens in those states have the right under state constitutions to exercise free speech rights in shopping malls. Our precious right to free speech should not vary from state to state, but if there is no alternative, then our right should be restored one state at a time.

Endnotes

1. 391 U.S. 308 (1968).
2. 308 F. Supp. 128, at 130.
3. 446 F.2d 545.
4. 407 U.S. 551 (June 22, 1972).
5. *Marsh v. Alabama,* 326 U.S. 501 (1946).

Chapter Eleven

The Second Boston Tea Party

"Where lies the final harbor?"

—Herman Melville in *Moby Dick*.

In December of 1979, in an act of unprovoked aggression, the Soviet Union invaded Afghanistan. On January 9, 1980, in protest of the Soviet invasion, Thomas W. "Teddy" Gleason, president of the International Longshoremen's Association (ILA) ordered its members to stop handling cargoes arriving from or destined for the Soviet Union. The order was effective on grain, food and other cargo. The ILA union controlled all East Coast and Gulf Coast ports, from New England to Texas. Rank and file union members supported the boycott. Gleason announced that the decision was made necessary by the demands of the workers. He said:

> "It is their will to refuse to work Russian vessels and Russian cargoes under present

conditions of the world. People are upset
and they refuse to continue business as
usual so long the Russians insist on being
international bully boys."

Thomas W. Gleason shown wearing his ILA tie pin.

The ILA President

ILA President Gleason wears a diamond studded "ILA" tiepin, which he, jokingly, claims stands for "I Love America." Gleason was born in 1900 and began working on the docks at age fifteen. He has seen the union survive wildcat strikes, riots, boycotts and racketeering scandals. In 1915, he dropped out of school and began working on the docks for ten cents an hour. In 1932, he was blacklisted for union activity, which was not then protected by federal law. After the National Labor Relations Act was passed as a part of the New Deal, Gleason returned to the docks and was elected a union organizer. He led wildcat strikes in 1946, 1949 and 1951, each time winning additional benefits for the union.

Gleason rose through the ranks to become president in 1963. He shaped an unruly mob of workers into a labor organization strong enough to influence international politics and brought stability to a strike-prone industry.

Allied International

Allied International is an American company that imports Russian wood products into the United States. Allied contracted with the Waterman Steamship Lines to deliver goods from Leningrad to Boston. As a result of the ILA boycott, Allied's shipments were completely disrupted. Allied was forced to renegotiate its Russian contracts, reducing its purchases significantly.

In Federal Court in Boston

Allied sued the ILA in the federal court in Boston, because its members refused to unload Allied's ships. Allied claimed that the boycott was illegal under the labor laws and interfered with Allied's contractual rights. The court dismissed Allied's case holding that the boycott was purely political, a primary boycott of Russian goods and protected by the First Amendment's right to free speech and association.[1] Judge Walter Skinner stated:

> "I am presented here, however, with political activity in the sense of a direct political protest against the Soviet Union's foreign policy. While commerce between Allied and the Soviet Union and, ultimately, the American people is being restrained by the ILA's refusal to handle certain cargo, this refusal is wholly politically oriented with no apparent economic benefit accruing to the union or its members.

> *   *   *

> Allied is still free to unload its ships by non-union personnel. ILA members have not boycotted any ships not involved in trade with the Soviet Union, including those ships owned by carriers who maintain Russian trade elsewhere.

> *   *   *

> A mere refusal to deal cannot consti-
> tute an interference as every worker may
> decline to offer his services just as every
> buyer may decide not to purchase."

The court of appeals reversed the dismissal and ruled that the boycott was not protected by the First Amendment.[2] The dispute was a labor issue, said the court, and the rights of free speech and association did not apply. The Supreme Court agreed to hear the case.

The First Boston Tea Party

The Boston Tea Party took place on December 16, 1773. The object of that protest was an overseas power, Britain. The issue was the British tax on tea. A group of forty to fifty Boston patriots, including longshore-men, unloaded the cargo of tea into the Boston Harbor. As a result of the tea dumping, Britain closed the Port of Boston. The Boston Tea Party was one of the events which led to the American Revolution.

In the Highest Court

The U.S. Supreme Court heard arguments in the longshoremen's case but finally agreed with court of appeals. The case, the court decided, was a "labor law" matter and not a matter of free speech and association.[3] The court said that the U.S. labor laws applied, because an American union was refusing to unload an American ship. The court found that under the labor laws, the boycott was an illegal secondary boycott. A primary boycott, or strike, is when workers are protesting directly against a company because of that company's policies or actions. The labor law outlaws secondary boycotts. The court gave the First Amendment this consideration:

> "There are many ways in which a union and its individual members may express their opposition to Russian foreign policy without infringing upon the rights of others."

There were also other ways that the citizens of Boston could have protested the British tax on tea without infringing on the rights of others. Consider the harm suffered by the tea drinkers in Boston, as well as the company that imported the tea. If the current labor laws had been in effect in 1773, the Boston Tea Party would have been illegal as a secondary boycott. The patriots who dumped the tea into the Boston harbor were not protesting against the tea company or the tea importer. They were, as here, protesting against the policies of a distant government. If those protesting the British tax on tea had decided to write letters to the editor instead of making an effective protest, we might still be part of the British Empire. Those colonial Americans would have wanted citizens of their new nation to have the right to protest against a government's oppression by means of a secondary boycott.

The First Amendment provides that "Congress shall pass no law abridging the freedom of speech, or of the press; or the right of the people peaceably to assemble." Congress passed the labor laws. The extent to which these laws conflict with the right to free speech, to protest, render them unconstitutional.

A political protest is a First Amendment protected activity. The Supreme Court has ruled, in other cases, that symbolic speech, such as the wearing of black armbands in protest of war, is protected speech.

The ILA boycott was the only *effective* way that the union could protest. Does the Constitution only protect *ineffective* means of protest?

The Founding Fathers would have been revolted by this *unanimous* Supreme Court ruling. At least one judge, Boston federal court Judge Walter Skinner, could separate free speech rights from union activities and labor laws.

Epilogue

After the Supreme Court ruling, Judge Skinner held a trial on the damages that Allied suffered because of the boycott. The court ruled that the union must pay about nine million dollars for the damages that the shipping firm suffered.

This damages award is one of the largest ever imposed against a labor union. The courts have punished a labor union for acting in a patriotic protest, one that should have had the full support of the country. Since the judge who first heard the case believed the union's activities were legal, the union should not have to suffer damages because the judge "erred."

ILA president Gleason has announced that he will retire from office in 1987 after twenty-four years of service. The boycott of Russian ships, that he started, lasted just over a year. The boycott began while Jimmy Carter was President of the United States. Gleason lifted the boycott at President Reagan's request, not under a court order.

Endnotes

1. 492 F. Supp. 334 (1980).
2. 640 F.2d 1368 (1981).
3. 456 U.S. 212 (1982).

PART 4
Equal Protection

Chapter Twelve

Once a Slave

"There is one thing stronger than all the armies in the world: and that is an idea whose time has come."

—Victor Hugo

Dred Scott was born in 1797 in Southampton County, Virginia, and became the property of Peter Blow. In 1827, he moved to St. Louis with the Blow family. Following the death of his owner in 1832, he became the property of Blow's daughter Elizabeth. The next year Elizabeth Blow sold Dred Scott to Dr. John Emerson, an assistant surgeon in the Army, for $500. Scott ran away but was recaptured.

The Missouri Compromise

In 1834, Dr. Emerson was ordered to duty at Fort Armstrong in Rock Island, Illinois, a free state, and Scott accompanied him there. The Army transferred

Dr. Emerson to Fort Snelling in 1836, and he, again, took Dred Scott with him.

Fort Snelling was then in the Wisconsin Territory and is now in Minnesota. Under the Missouri Compromise, slavery was outlawed in this northern part of the Louisiana territory. The Missouri Compromise of 1820 provided that slavery was permitted in the Louisiana Territory from Missouri southward and that slavery was prohibited north of Missouri.

On Free Soil

Dred Scott remained on free soil for about five years, from 1834 until 1839. In 1835, he met Harriet, a slave of Major Taliaferro, who was in the U.S. Army. In that year, Major Taliaferro took Harriet to Fort Snelling and kept her as a slave until 1836, when he sold her to Dr. Emerson. In that year, Emerson permitted Dred Scott to marry Harriet.

Dr. Emerson left Fort Snelling in 1838, unaccompanied by the Scotts. The Scotts raised two daughters, Eliza and Lizzie. Eliza was born in about 1843, aboard the steamboat Gipsey on the Mississippi River. She was born north of the northern border of Missouri, in free territory. Lizzie was born in about 1850. The Scott family departed from the Wisconsin Territory, after Emerson, and, probably, went back to St. Louis.

Dred Scott's New Owner

In 1843, Dr. Emerson died and his widow, Irene Sanford Emerson, inherited his slaves. Mrs. Emerson did what many slaveowners did in those days; she hired out her slaves to various families who needed servants. Then, in the mid-1840s, she moved to New York and did not take Dred Scott, or any members of his family, with her. She left him in St. Louis with Henry and Taylor Blow, two sons of Scott's original owner.

Henry Blow was then in his thirties, a lawyer and a successful businessman. He ran a railroad and was active in lead mining. Henry Blow was also active in the Whig Party, a party which opposed the extension of slavery in the territories. Blow later organized the Free-Soil movement in Missouri and became a Republican.

The Lawsuit is Commenced

As an opponent of slavery, Henry Blow wanted Scott freed, and, in 1846, he financed a suit in the Missouri courts to have Scott declared to be a free man. The lawsuit was Blow's idea, but Scott signed the necessary papers.

The 1846 lawsuit was filed against Emerson's estate. Scott claimed that he became a free man when he accompanied his master into Illinois and the Wisconsin Territory, and his status could not be reversed by his return to Missouri.

The aim of the lawsuit, although specifically seeking

Scott's freedom, was to undercut slavery in the territories. This was important at the time, because the West was opening up for settlement, and many slaveowners were bringing slaves with them into the new territory. From 1846 to 1848, the Mexican-American War raged. At the end of the war, the United States expanded its territory to California. By this time, the question of slavery in the new territories became one of the major issues of the nation.

Mrs. Emerson did not want to retain Scott as a slave. She apparently did not believe in slavery. A few years later, she married Calvin Clifford Chaffee, a radical antislavery Congressman from Massachusetts. She could easily have signed papers emancipating Scott, but she did not.

In 1850, Scott won a jury verdict in his favor, but the case was appealed. After Scott won in the lower court, he came under control of the county sheriff, who hired him out for five dollars a month. During the appeal, Scott was everybody's slave and nobody's slave.

The Missouri Supreme Court in 1852 ruled that Scott became a slave when he reentered Missouri. After losing his case, Scott continued to work on odd jobs and was occasionally farmed out. But, he became an important person because of his lawsuit. Antislavery people were moving into the territories and were looking for a way to revive his lawsuit.

Into the Federal Courts

On November 2, 1853, Scott became the plaintiff in

a new lawsuit brought into federal court in St. Louis. Mrs. Emerson transferred title to Scott over to her brother John Sanford, so the case became known as *Dred Scott v. Sandford.* Harriet Scott and Lizzie and Eliza Scott were also named as plaintiffs. They sued for their liberty and for damages for being wrongfully held as slaves. The Scott's lawsuit sought $16,500 for damages. The case was tried before an all-white jury, who ruled in Mr. Sanford's favor, and who determined that the Scotts were lawfully his property.

In 1854, Senator Douglas of Illinois led the fight to pass the Kansas-Nebraska Act. This law, based on the principle of popular sovereignty, provided that the settlers in these new territories would determine the slavery issue by an election. Meanwhile, slaveowners were free to move into the territories. The importance of Dred Scott's case was growing.

In the Supreme Court

The *Dred Scott* case was argued two times before the Supreme Court. It was first argued in February of 1856, but the court could not reach a decision on the question of whether Scott was a citizen of the United States and entitled to file suit in federal court. Four justices leaned one way, four the other; the swing justice, Justice Nelson, thought it best to set the case for reargument. Reargument was set for December, after the presidential election between James M. Buchanan, John C. Fremont and ex-President Millard Fillmore. Justice McLean wanted the court to rule early in 1856, so that he could write a stinging dissent to the court's upholding of slavery and run for president himself.

DRED SCOTT.   PHOTOGRAPHED BY FITZGIBBON, OF ST. LOUIS.

Photoengraving of Dred Scott, courtesy of the Library of Congress.

HIS WIFE, HARRIET.   PHOTOGRAPHED BY FITZGIBBON, OF ST. LOUIS.

Photoengraving of Harriet Scott, courtesy of the Library of Congress.

Photoengraving of Eliza and Lizzie Scott, courtesy of Library of Congress.

In mid-December, the court heard four days of oral argument. The justices did not meet to discuss the case until February 1857. One of the justices, John Catron of Tennessee, took the highly unusual step of writing to his old friend, President-elect Buchanan, for advice. Buchanan tried to steer clear of the decision and, in his inaugural address, said that the nation should support whatever decision at which the Supreme Court arrived.

Two days after Buchanan was sworn in as President, the Supreme Court announced its decision against Dred Scott. All nine justices wrote separate opinions, seven in favor of the decision and two in dissent; all totalled, the justices wrote 250 pages explaining their ruling. Justice Taney wrote that black slaves and their descendants could not become citizens of the United States and ruled that the Missouri Compromise was unconstitutional.[1] The court ruled that slavery could not be prohibited in the territories. This decision widened the breach between the northern and southern states and was one of the causes of the Civil War.

Justice Curtis, in his dissent, pointed out the Taney was simply wrong:

> "At the time of the ratification of the Articles of Confederation (1781), all free native-born inhabitants of the States of New Hampshire, Massachusetts, New York, New Jersey, and North Carolina, though descended from African slaves, were not only citizens of those States, but such of these as had the other necessary qualifications possessed the franchise of electors, on equal terms with other citizens."

The Justices as Politicians

Who were the justices and where were they from?
Taney, the Chief Justice, was from Maryland, a slave
state. Four other justices were from slave states: Wayne
of Georgia, Catron of Tennessee, Daniel of Virginia
and Campbell of Alabama. Only three of these southern Justices agreed that Negroes of slave ancestry
could not become citizens.

All of the Southern justices along with Nelson of
New York decided that Scott's status depended upon
the law of Missouri. The five Southerners, along with
Grier of Pennsylvania, ruled that the Missouri Compromise was unconstitutional because it deprived citizens
of the right to take property (slaves) into the territories. The dissenters, McLean and Curtis, argued that
Scott was a citizen, that Missouri law did not control
his status and that Congress had a constitutional right
to prohibit slavery from a territory.

Epilogue

John Sanford died before the case was announced.
Mrs. Emerson and her husband, Dr. Chaffee, transferred their rights in the Scotts to Taylor Blow, the son
of Scott's original owner. Blow emancipated the Scotts
in May 1857. Scott was quoted as saying that his lawsuit had brought him a "heap o' trouble" and that had
he known that it would last so long he never would
have brought it in the first case. Scott became a porter
in a St. Louis hotel. September 17, 1858 Scott died of
tuberculosis in St. Louis. Henry Blow paid his funeral
expenses.

For the nation, the court's decision was an unmitigated disaster. The decision could be changed only by a constitutional amendment (an impossibility given Southern opposition), by the court itself (not likely) or by force.

The case, especially Justice Taney's opinion, inflamed the North. The decision also split the Democratic Party. "Popular sovereignty," which had been advocated by Senator Douglas to let the states decide on slavery by themselves, had been ruled unconstitutional. The Northern Democrats could not agree with the South's demands for slavery in the territories. With the collapse of Douglas' compromise, Abraham Lincoln and the Republicans gained the White House.

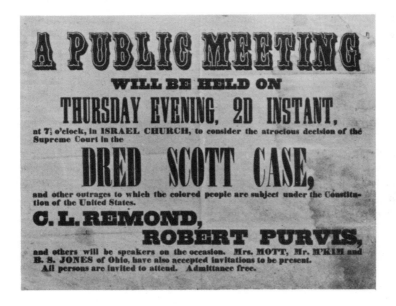

Poster announcing public meeting to discuss Dred Scott decision.

The *Dred Scott* decision, while not the sole cause of the Civil War, certainly contributed to its inevitability. After the Civil War, the Thirteenth and Fourteenth Amendments were passed, which formally overturned the Supreme Court's ruling in the *Dred Scott* case. Those amendments outlawed slavery and gave Negroes the right to vote.

Endnotes

1. 19 How. 691 (1857).

Chapter Thirteen

Off Broadway

"In giving freedom to the slave, we assure freedom to the free."

—Abraham Lincoln

"I desired to find an entrance to the palace."

—Victor Hugo in *Ruy Blas*

At 10:00 Saturday morning November 22, 1879, a light-skinned young woman bought two tickets for that afternoon's matinee at the Grand Opera House in New York City.[1] The afternoon performance of Victor Hugo's *Ruy Blas* featured Edwin Booth, brother of infamous John Wilkes Booth. A few months earlier, a madman had attempted to shoot Booth during a performance of *Richard II*. Because of the publicity of the shooting attempt and because of the Thanksgiving crowds, the Grand Opera House was jammed.

Ruy Blas is a play in which the main character, Blas, falls in love with a woman of royal blood who lives in the palace. When it is found out that he is a commoner, their relationship ends.

At 1:30, the young lady and her boyfriend, William R. Davis, Jr., a tall, dark, handsome and well-dressed escort of age twenty-six, arrived at the Grand Opera. Samuel Singleton, the Grand Opera doorkeeper refused admittance to the couple saying "these tickets are no good." The doorkeeper refused them admittance, because Mr. Davis was a Negro. Had he known that Davis' girlfriend was one-eighth Negro, he would have refused her admittance as well.

Mr. Davis was offered a refund for his ticket, but he refused it. He saw a small white boy standing near the theater. Davis gave him a dollar plus ten cents for his trouble and had him purchase two more tickets for the matinee. Again, Sam Singleton refused Davis admission but admitted his girlfriend. Davis refused to move out of the entrance. Singleton took hold of Davis and forced him out of the theatre and called a policeman for assistance. When Davis protested to the policeman, the officer told Davis that the managers of the theatre, Poole and Donnelly, did not admit colored people and told Davis that he had better go away. "Perhaps the managers do not," said Davis, "but the laws of the country do." He announced that he would seek their enforcement at once.

Davis and his girlfriend left the theater and went to a matinee performance at another theater.

The Grand Opera House.

The Fourteenth Amendment

After the Civil War, Congress and the States passed the Fourteenth Amendment, giving blacks all rights secured by their fellow citizens, and prohibited the states from depriving Negroes of equal protection under the laws. The amendment also gave Congress the power to enforce the terms of the amendment by appropriate legislation. To enforce the Fourteenth Amendment, Congress passed the Civil Rights Law, which forbade racial discrimination in places of public accommodation, including theaters, restaurants and hotels.

William R. Davis, Jr.

Davis, born a slave in South Carolina, became free
with Lincoln's Emancipation Proclamation. He moved
to New York City, where he resided at No. 109 West
Twenty-Seventh Street. He was employed as the business agent of the *Progressive American*, a weekly
newspaper devoted to the advancement of black Americans. It was undoubtedly his dedication to this cause
that led him to make a criminal complaint.

The Criminal Complaint

After consulting with the United States attorney,
Mr. Fiero, on Monday, November 24th, Davis filed a
criminal complaint. Fiero recommended that Davis file
a civil suit against the theatre. However, Davis had
done this before, in September 1875, after he was denied admission to Booth's Theatre. That case was dismissed because Davis's witnesses failed to appear.

On December 9th, Singleton was indicted. It was the
first criminal proceeding in New York State under the
Civil Rights Law. The case was heard on January 14,
1880. The attorney for Singleton, Louis Post, argued
that the Civil Rights Act was unconstitutional, because
it interfered with the rights of citizens and their private property. The judge referred the issue to the Circuit Court, which could not reach a decision, and referred the case to the Supreme Court.

The Highest Court's Ruling

On Monday, October 15, 1883, the Supreme Court ruled that the Civil Rights Act was unconstitutional.[2] Justice Joseph Bradley wrote the opinion for the court. In his opinion he wrote:

> "Why may not Congress . . . enact a code of laws for the enforcement and vindication of all rights of life, liberty, and property? . . . . [Because i]t is repugnant to the Tenth Amendment of the Consititution, which declares that powers not delegated to the United States by the Constitution, nor prohibited by it to the States, are reserved to the States respectively or to the people."

Justice Bradley, and a majority of the court, held that the Fourteenth Amendment to the Constitution gives the Congress little power to legislate. However, that amendment provides that no State shall deny "any person within its jurisdiction the equal protection of the laws." The amendment further provides that "Congress shall have the power to enforce, by appropriate legislation, the provisions of this article." Under the laws of New York, William Davis should have had an equal right to attend a performance at the Grand Opera House. However, the laws of New York did not protect him. He purchased a ticket, but the New York police were called to evict him, not to help him. Congress passed the Civil Rights Laws for this very reason: in order to protect the citizen's right to equal protection of the laws and for equal access to places of public accommodation, including theaters and hotels.

Once Davis acquired a ticket for admission, it was a breach of contract for the theater to deny his admission. Justice Bradley is saying that the State of New York had nothing to do with the transaction. However, New York police were called to the scene. The State of New York was obligated by the Fourteenth Amendment to see to it that Mr. Davis' rights were protected. Instead, New York's finest ejected Davis from the theater, when they should have escorted him in.

The Tenth Amendment is rarely relied on. The Fourteenth Amendment was passed after the Civil War to remove all vestiges of slavery. The amendment was passed by three-quarters of the States and by Congress, and represented the will of the people.

Further, since the Fourteenth Amendment was enacted after the Tenth Amendment, any conflict between the two should be resolved in favor of the latter amendment. The Supreme Court's finding that the Civil Rights Act was unconstitutional ignores the meaning and intent of the Fourteenth Amendment and was an attempt to overturn the outcome of the Civil War.

Justice John Marshall Harlan of Kentucky, the only Southerner on the Court, wrote the sole dissent:

> "Today, it is the colored race which is denied, by corporations and individuals wielding public authority, rights fundamental in their freedom and citizenship. At some future time, it may be that some other race will fall under the ban

of race discrimination. If the constitutional amendments be enforced, according
to the intent with which, as I conceive,
they were adopted, there cannot be in
this republic, any class of human beings
in practical subjection to another class."

Justice Harlan penned his famous dissent with
Justice Taney's inkwell. Taney had authored the majority opinion in the *Dred Scott case.*

The *New York Times* quoted Justice Harlan:[3]

"[U]nder ordinary circumstances and in
an ordinary case he [a justice] should
hesitate to set up his individual opinion
in opposition to that of his eight collea-
gues, but in view of what he thought the
people of the country wished to accomplish, what they tried to accomplish, and
what they believed they had accom-
plished by means of this legislation, he
must express his dissent from the opinion
of the court."

Frederick Douglass, a former slave and civil rights
advocate during the era of this decision said:[4]

"The future historian will turn to the
year 1883 to find the most flagrant example of national deterioration. Here he
will find the Supreme Court of the nation reversing the action of the Government, defeating the manifest purpose of
the Constitution, nullifying the Fourteenth Amendment, and placing itself on

the side of prejudice, proscription, and persecution.

Whatever this Supreme Court may have been in the past, or may by the Constitution have been intended to be, it has, since the days of the Dred Scott decision, been wholly under the influence of slave power, and its decisions have been dictated by that power rather than by what seemed to be sound and established rules of legal interpretation.

Although we had, in other days, seen this court bend and twist the law to the will and interest of slave power, it was supposed that by the late war and the great fact that slavery was abolished, and the further fact that the members of the bench were now appointed by a Republican administration, the spirit as well as the body had been exorcised. Hence the decision in question came to the black man as a painful and bewildering surprise. It was a blow from an unsuspected quarter. The surrender of the national capital to Jefferson Davis in time of the war could hardly have caused a greater shock."

Endnotes

1. Some details were provided by the *New York Times,* November 25, 1879.

2. 109 U.S. 3 (1883).

3. *New York Times,* October 16, 1883.

4. *Life and Times of Frederick Douglass,* MacMillan Publishing Co., New York: 1962.

Chapter Fourteen

American Apartheid

"Each time a man stands up for an idea, or acts to improve the lot others, or strikes out against injustice, he sends forth tiny ripple of hope . . . those ripples build a current that can sweep down the mightiest walls of oppression and resistance."

—Robert F. Kennedy in Capetown, South Afica

"Jim Crow" was the name of a song sung by Thomas Rice in a Negro minstrel show before the Civil War. Thomas Rice was a white actor who, in black face played the part of Jim Crow. During the minstrel show, he sang, "Wheel about, turn about, do just so. Everytime I wheel about I jump Jim Crow."

Jim Crow came to signify white dominance over blacks, and laws that required segregation of blacks and whites became known as Jim Crow laws. The first Jim Crow law, requiring railroads to carry Negroes in separate cars, was passed by Florida in 1887. The rest of the Southern states joined by passing similar laws.

Louisiana passed its Jim Crow law regarding railroads
in 1890, even though Negroes in New Orleans had
organized against passage of the bill.

The black community in New Orleans had a
heritage of several generations of freedom and a high
degree of literacy. Louisiana had sixteen black senators
and representatives at the time. A group called the E-
qual Rights Association of Louisiana Against Class
Legislation protested against the law as "unconstitutional, unamerican, unjust, dangerous and against sound
public policy." Nevertheless, the Assembly passed the
bill and the governor signed it into law. The act was
titled "An Act to promote the comfort of passengers,"
and required railroads to provide equal but separate accommodations for colored and white passengers.

A Test Case

In 1891, a group of eighteen black men formed a
"Citizens Committee to Test the Constitutionality of
the Separate Car Law." Within five weeks, they raised
$1,500 for a test case. The committee hired Albion
Tourgée as counsel in the case. Tourgée was a well-
known, light-colored black attorney, novelist and former North Carolina judge. Tourgée recommended that
a light-skinned Negro be used for the test case.

Railroad officials were cooperative because segregation was inconvenient and expensive for them. The
first railroad approached, admitted that it did not enforce the Jim Crow law.

The committee members finally agreed that a white

passenger should object to the presence of a Negro in a "white" car, that the conductor should send the black passenger to the second class car and that the passenger should refuse to go. For the first test case, Daniel Desdunes bought a ticket on the Louisville & Nashville Railroad from New Orleans to Mobile, Alabama. When the matter was brought to court, the Louisiana judge ruled that the Jim Crow law was unconstitutional, as applied to interstate passengers. However, the law was still valid as to intrastate trains which most blacks used.

Homer Plessy

The committee looked for another plaintiff for a new test case and chose Homer Plessy; he was an octoroon: seven-eighths white and one-eighth black. The East Louisiana Railroad had been informed of the plan and agreed to cooperate. Plessy took a seat in the white coach. The conductor requested that he move to the Negro car, which he refused to do. Detective Christopher Cain arrested Plessy and charged him with violating the separate car law.

Tourgée entered a plea before Judge John H. Ferguson of the Criminal District Court for the Parish of New Orleans, arguing that the law Mr. Plessy allegedly violated was invalid, because it conflicted with the Constitution of the United States. Ferguson ruled against Plessy, and the case of *Plessy v. Ferguson* was born. Plessy was fined twenty-five dollars.

Tourgée argued:

"[T]he statute in question establishes an

insidious distinction and discrimination
between citizens of the United States,
based on race, which is obnoxious to the
fundamental principles of national citizenship, perpetuates involuntary servitude,
as regards citizens of the colored race,
under the merest pretense of promoting
the comfort of passengers on railway
trains, and in further respects abridges
the privileges and immunities of the citizens of the United States, and the rights
secured by the thirteenth and fourteenth
amendments of the federal constitution."

An Appeal

The State Supreme Court granted a hearing. The
Chief Justice of this court was Francis Nicholls, who
had signed the Jim Crow act into law as governor of
Louisiana two years earlier. The case was assigned to
Judge Fenner. Judge Fenner ruled that "separate but e-
qual" was a proper law, since the Fourteenth Amendment provided for equal protection under the laws, not
undivided protection. Since the statute specifically
required equal accommodations, it complied with the
Constitution. Judge Fenner relied on *Roberts v. City
of Boston*, which upheld segregated public schools in
Boston:

"In a case which arose as far back as
1849, the supreme court of Massachusetts,
through its great chief justice, Shaw, considered the subject, saying: 'Conceding,

therefore, in the fullest manner, that colored persons, the descendants of Africans, are entitled by law to equal rights, constitutional and political, civil and social, the question then arises whether the regulations in question which provide for separate schools for colored children, is a violation of any of these rights.

*   *   *

This prejudice, if it exists, is not created by law, and it cannot be changed by law."

Judge Nicholls granted Plessy's petition for a writ of error. This permitted him to appeal the case to the Supreme Court of the United States.

Plessy v. Ferguson at the Supreme Court

When Tourgée argued the case before the Supreme Court, he asked the members of the court to imagine how they would have felt had they been ordered into a Jim Crow car. "What humiliation, what rage would then fill the judicial mind!" he argued. The true intent of the Louisiana statute was apparent, Tourgée contended, because it did not apply "to nurses attending children of the other race."

Tourgée argued:

"The exemption of nurses shows that the real evil lies not in the color of the

skin but in the relation the colored person sustains to the whole. If he is a de-
pendent, it may be endured: if he is not,
his presence is insufferable.   Instead of
being intended to promote the *general*
comfort and moral well-being, this act is
plainly and evidently intended to promote
the happiness of one class by asserting its
supremacy and the inferiority of another
class. Justice is pictured blind and her
daughter, the Law, ought at least to be
color-blind.

*   *   *

Why not require all colored people to
walk on one side of the street and all
whites on the other? . . . One side of the
street may be just as good as the other . .
. . The question is not as to the equality
of the privileges enjoyed, but *the right of
the State to label one citizen as white and
another as colored* in the common enjoy-
ment of the public highway."

During the two years that *Plessy v. Ferguson* remained before the Supreme Court, new segregation
laws were passed and lynchings had increased. Two
states had already disenfranchised the Negro, and several others were planning to take that unconstitutional
step.

Albion Tourgee the attorney who represented Homer Plessy.

Separate but Equal

On Monday, May 18, 1896, Justice Henry Billings
Brown of Michigan, by way of Massachusetts, delivered
the opinion of the court.[1] Only Justice Harlan dissented.
Like Justice Fenner of the State Supreme Court,
Justice Brown depended on the case of *Roberts v. City
of Boston*, a case decided in 1849, before the Civil War
and, more importantly, before the Fourteenth Amendment to the Constitution, which guaranteed citizens
"equal protection of the laws." He contended that Congress, which had passed the Fourteenth Amendment,
continued to approve of the segregated school system
in the District of Columbia and, therefore, must have
felt that segregation was consistent with the amendment. Separate but equal became the law of the land.

Epilogue

Separate but equal remained the law of the land
until *Brown v. Board of Education*[2] decided that "separate" is "inherently unequal" in 1954. *Plessy v. Ferguson* had remained the law of the land for exactly fifty-eight years, from May 18, 1896 to May 17, 1954.
During those fifty-eight years, American Apartheid
reined supreme as Homer Plessy's case was cited in
cases regarding every conceivable type of racial discrimination.

Endnotes

1. 163 U.S. 537 (1896).
2. 347 U.S. 483 (1954).

Chapter Fifteen

The Summer of '42

"The great strength of the totalitarian state is that it forces those who fear it to imitate it."

—Adolf Hitler

Fred and Ida

Fred was twenty-three years of age in 1942. He had tried to enlist in the Army the year before but was rejected because he suffered from a stomach ulcer. Fred studied to be a welder and, before Pearl Harbor was attacked, worked in shipyards in California building our Navy's flotilla. He was a patriotic American, a native-born Californian. He lived in the same house in Oakland until he went to Los Angeles to attend college. As soon as he turned twenty-one, he proudly voted for Franklin Roosevelt, who was seeking re-election for an unprecedented third term as president.

Fred fell in love with an Italian girl, Ida Boitano.

He spent most of his free time with her. Fred had one problem: his parents were born in Japan. Even though Fred Korematsu was a native-born U.S. citizen, he was considered to be "of Japanese ancestry." In December, 1941, Japan nearly destroyed the American naval fleet at Pearl Harbor. Rumors of an imminent invasion of the West Coast made Californians anxious. Now and then, Japanese submarines were sighted off of the coast.

An anti-Japanese hysteria was brewing in California, Oregon and Washington. Many Americans of Japanese ancestry were fired from their jobs. Fred Korematsu was one of them.

The United States declared war on Japan, Italy and Germany soon after Pearl Harbor, but those of Japanese ancestry were treated far worse than Italian-Americans and German-Americans. There were too many Americans of German and Italian ancestry, and they had intermarried with "true" Americans more than the Japanese. Italians and Germans looked like Americans; they were fair skinned, while Japanese-Americans looked like foreigners. And they were treated like foreigners, enemy aliens.

The War, The Panic

In late November of 1941, shortly before Pearl Harbor was attacked, President Roosevelt, Korematsu's candidate, ordered the names and addresses of all American and foreign born Japanese persons to be compiled. Historian and former Congressman John Toland reports that the secrecy of the census was violated in order to produce the list of addresses of Japanese living in the United States. The list was compiled in one week and was on the president's desk before Pearl Harbor was attacked.

After Pearl Harbor, the Pacific Coast was shelled at Santa Barbara, California and at Seaside, Oregon. Near Seattle, a Japanese submarine sank a ship and attacked Vancouver Island. The Japanese occupied Kiska Island in the Aleutian Islands and bombed the U.S. Naval base in nearby Dutch Harbor.

On December 7th, as Pearl Harbor was being attacked, the Japanese simultaneously struck at the Malay Peninsula, Hong Kong, Wake and Midway Islands and the Philippines. The next day, they invaded Thailand. Within a week, Guam fell, and, on Christmas Day, the Japanese captured Wake Island and Hong Kong. General MacArthur was forced to evacuate Manila. MacArthur's troops had become isolated by rapidly advancing Japanese forces and suffered one of the worst American defeats of the war. In February, the Americans were defeated in the Battle of the Java Sea and lost thirteen ships. At that time, the U.S. position in the Pacific looked very bleak.

Because of a real fear of invasion based on Japanese military successes, and because of racial differences, there was a growing public clamor for action to be taken against the Japanese who were living in the United States. Earl Warren, then attorney general of California, and planning to run for governor of the state, prepared arguments in favor of imposing restrictions on the Japanese-Americans living on the West Coast.

Warren painted a threatening picture. With use of color-coded, maps he showed the pattern of Japanese land ownership near American Army and Naval bases. The Army and Navy made recommendations, which along with Warren's maps, were submitted to the President.

Similar maps of Italian-American land ownership were never prepared but would have shown an equally threatening picture. Italian restaurants "surround" San Francisco Bay and would appear from a color-coded map to be part of a grand strategy to capture the bay area.

It was during this period that President Roosevelt signed Executive Order 9066, which gave the secretary of war and the military commanders the power to exclude any person from designated areas in order to secure national defense objectives against sabotage and espionage. The military commander for the western states, Lieutenant General J. L. DeWitt, took full advantage of the powers that the executive order gave him.

General DeWitt

Lieutenant General DeWitt was designated the military commander for the westernmost parts of the United States. President Roosevelt signed Executive Order 9066 on February 19, 1942. General DeWitt wasted little time, and, on March 2nd, he issued Public Proclamation Number One which established Military Areas Numbers One and Two. Military Area Number One encompassed the western halves of California, Oregon and Washington and the southern half of Arizona. Military Area Number Two was the eastern remainder of California.

DeWitt's plan for the Japanese living in these newly designated "military areas" became apparent. On March 24, 1942, from his comfortable headquarters for the Western Defense Command in San Francisco, General DeWitt issued his third public proclamation. This proclamation announced a curfew for enemy aliens (Germans, Italians and Japanese) and for U.S. citizens of Japanese ancestry. DeWitt imposed a strict curfew between the hours of 8:00 p.m. and 6:30 a.m. During those hours Japanese-Americans (and enemy aliens) had to remain in their homes. Outside of those hours, persons of Japanese ancestry were permitted to work, if anyone would hire them, but could not otherwise stray more than five miles from their residences. If they lived in Oakland, they could not go to San Francisco without running afoul of the military proclamation.

In addition, the proclamation prohibited Japanese-Americans from possessing firearms, short-wave radios, radio transmitters, signalling devices and cameras. In the next proclamation, DeWitt required enemy aliens and native-born Japanese-Americans to receive prior approval from the Army, before they could legally change their home addresses.

The Evacuation

Even before the curfew was imposed by General DeWitt, the U.S. Navy forcibly evicted 3,500 Japanese from Terminal Island in Los Angeles harbor. These civilians were fishermen, their families and local businessmen, but the Navy considered them a serious threat to national security. On February 25th, the Terminal Islanders were given forty-eight hours to leave the island. The residents were forced to sell their belong-

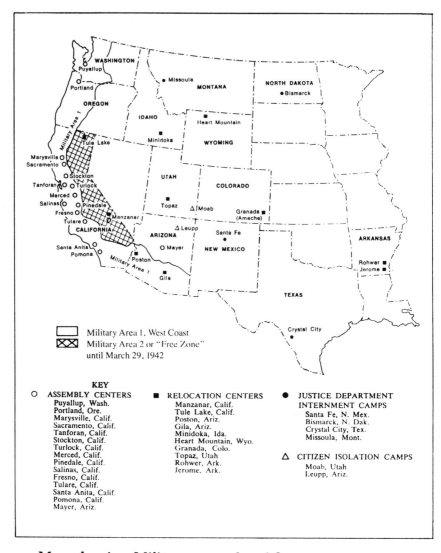

Map showing Military areas 1 and 2.

ings for a pittance, or to abandon them. After the evacuation, the island was littered with abandoned household appliances and furniture.

The next Japanese community to be evicted was another fishing village, Bainbridge Island in Puget Sound,
near Seattle. During the latter part of March, 1942, the
forty-five Japanese-American families who resided on
the island were forced to abandon their homes.

These evacuations sent shockwaves of panic through
the Japanese communities on the West Coast. Alien
fishermen were arrested by the military and sent to the
interior of the United States, to Bismark, North Dakota
and to other remote areas. American citizens of Japanese ancestry who were forced to evacuate their homes
either moved in with relatives or went to one of the
two new "voluntary" relocation centers: Manzanar in
the Owens Valley in California or the Northern
Colorado Indian Reservation in Arizona.

General DeWitt divided Military Area Number One
into ninety-nine zones and ordered the evacuation of
Japanese-Americans one zone at a time. The exclusion
orders were posted on telephone poles, on store fronts
and at bus stops. Fred Korematsu had lived his entire
life in Oakland at 10800 Edes Avenue. Civilian Exclusion Number Twenty-Seven made it illegal for him to
live in his own home.

The Korematsu Evacuation

In April, 1942, Fred Korematsu left home, telling his
family that he was going to start a home in Nevada.
At the time, Nevada was a legal place of residence for

persons of Japanese ancestry. Instead of going to Nevada, however, Fred stayed in Oakland to earn enough
money to take his girlfriend, Ida Boitano, with him to
the Midwest. Fred and Ida had made plans to marry
and dreamed of living a normal life together. But this
was not to be.

Fred Korematsu went from place to place, attempting to avoid arrest for violating the curfew and evacuation orders. He routinely violated the curfew by going
out with Ida after hours. He changed his name to
Clyde Sarah, because he thought that it sounded more
American, and underwent plastic surgery, so that his
face did not look Japanese. But, the operation performed on Korematsu in May in San Francisco was not
very successful: he still looked Japanese.

Fred lived in San Francisco for a few weeks while
his face healed from plastic surgery. He lived in
Oakland after noon on Thursday, May 7, 1942, the date
by which all Japanese-Americans were required to
evacuate. Fred Korematsu knew about the civilian exclusion order but disregarded it, because he wanted to
be with his friends, especially Ida. He felt that the exclusion order was illegal. Why did the order apply to
him and not to his Italian girlfriend? The United States
was at war against both Italy and Japan.

In order to avoid detection, and to prevent ostracism
when he moved east with Ida, Fred rented rooms
under his assumed name in two rooming houses in
Oakland, one at 1428 44th Avenue and the other near
the corner of Fruitvale and East 14th Street. Clyde
Sarah obtained a social security number and worked
for one week for the Anderson Trailer Center on Mac-
Arthur Boulevard and for a month for the Trailer

Fred Korematsu in 1942, courtesy of Mr. Korematsu.

**WESTERN DEFENSE COMMAND AND FOURTH ARMY
WARTIME CIVIL CONTROL ADMINISTRATION**

Presidio of San Francisco, California

INSTRUCTIONS

TO ALL PERSONS OF

JAPANESE

ANCESTRY

LIVING IN THE FOLLOWING AREA:

All of that portion of the County of Alameda, State of California, within that boundary beginning at the point at which the southerly limits of the City of Berkeley meet San Francisco Bay; thence easterly and following the southerly limits of said city to College Avenue; thence southerly on College Avenue to Broadway; thence southerly on Broadway to the southerly limits of the City of Oakland; thence following the limits of said city westerly and northerly, and following the shoreline of San Francisco Bay to the point of beginning.

Pursuant to the provisions of Civilian Exclusion Order No. 27, this Headquarters, dated April 30, 1942, all persons of Japanese ancestry, both alien and non-alien, will be evacuated from the above area by 12 o'clock noon, P.W.T., Thursday May 7, 1942.

No Japanese person living in the above area will be permitted to change residence after 12 o'clock noon, P.W.T., Thursday, April 30, 1942, without obtaining special permission from the representative of the Commanding General, Northern California Sector, at the Civil Control Station located at:

530 Eighteenth Street,
Oakland, California.

Such permits will only be granted for the purpose of uniting members of a family, or in cases of grave emergency.

The Civil Control Station is equipped to assist the Japanese population affected by this evacuation in the following ways:

1. Give advice and instructions on the evacuation.

2. Provide services with respect to the management, leasing, sale, storage or other disposition of most kinds of property, such as real estate, business and professional equipment, household goods, boats, automobiles and livestock.

3. Provide temporary residence elsewhere for all Japanese in family groups.

4. Transport persons and a limited amount of clothing and equipment to their new residence.

Poster giving instructions to persons of Japanese ancestry.

Headquarters
Western Defense Command
and Fourth Army
Presidio of San Francisco, California
April 30, 1942

Civilian Exclusion Order No. 27

1. Pursuant to the provisions of Public Proclamations Nos. 1 and 2, this Headquarters, dated March 2, 1942, and March 16, 1942, respectively, it is hereby ordered that from and after 12 o'clock noon, P.W.T., of Thursday, May 7, 1942, all persons of Japanese ancestry, both alien and non-alien, be excluded from that portion of Military Area No. 1 described as follows:

   All of that portion of the County of Alameda, State of California, within that boundary beginning at the point at which the southerly limits of the City of Berkeley meet San Francisco Bay; thence easterly and following the southerly limits of said city to College Avenue; thence southerly on College Avenue to Broadway; thence southerly on Broadway to the southerly limits of the City of Oakland; thence following the limits of said city westerly and northerly, and following the shoreline of San Francisco Bay to the point of beginning.

2. A responsible member of each family, and each individual living alone, in the above described area will report between the hours of 8:00 A. M. and 5:00 P. M., Friday, May 1, 1942, or during the same hours on Saturday, May 2, 1942, to the Civil Control Station located at:

   530 Eighteenth Street
   Oakland, California.

3. Any person subject to this order who fails to comply with any of its provisions or with the provisions of published instructions pertaining hereto or who is found in the above area after 12 o'clock noon, P.W.T., of Thursday, May 7, 1942, will be liable to the criminal penalties provided by Public Law No. 503, 77th Congress, approved March 21, 1942 entitled "An Act to Provide a Penalty for Violation of Restrictions or Orders with Respect to Persons Entering, Remaining in, Leaving, or Committing any Act in Military Areas or Zones," and alien Japanese will be subject to immediate apprehension and internment.

4. All persons within the bounds of an established Assembly Center pursuant to instructions from this Headquarters are excepted from the provisions of this order while those persons are in such Assembly Center.

J. L. DeWitt
Lieutenant General, U. S. Army
Commanding

A typical order excluding Japanese-Americans from certain areas.

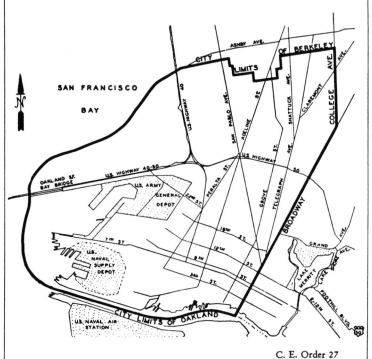

Map showing an exclusion area.

Center on MacArthur Boulevard and for a month for
the Trailer Company of America in Berkeley at 7th
and Gilman Streets.

Korematsu used ink remover to change the name on
his draft card to Clyde Sarah and to remove his race
and parents' place of birth from his birth certificate.

The pressure of being a fugitive, the fear of arrest
and the hatred he saw in the faces of white Americans,
was getting to him. He missed his family, and he hated
to see the white man who took over his father's nursery business. His family was in Tanforan, the assembly
center in Marin County, north of San Francisco.

On May 30, 1942, Fred was with Ida in San Leandro, a few miles south of Oakland. He told her that he
had quit his job at the trailer company and was going
to turn himself in. He told her that he would challenge
the evacuation order and that he would see her soon.
Fred Korematsu, whose only guilt was that his parents
were born in Japan, turned himself in at the San
Leandro Police Department.

The Confession

The San Leandro Police searched Korematsu and
had the Oakland Police search his small room off
Fruitvale Street. The police notified the Federal Bu-
reau of Investigation, which sent in Special Agent Oliver T. Mansfield to interview him. Fred Korematsu vol-
untarily gave the FBI a full statement. Based on his
"confession," a criminal information charge was filed
against him on June 12, 1942, and he was held without

bail until his trial on September 8, 1942.

Fred Korematsu spent the summer of 1942 interned at the Tanforan Assembly Center, awaiting his chance to prove that he was a patriotic American citizen.

The Trial

The federal government prosecuted Fred Korematsu for violating Civil Exclusion Order Thirty-Four, which applied to military zone thirty-four, San Leandro, California. At the trial, the federal prosecutor introduced the interview with Korematsu, the altered draft card and a certified copy of Korematsu's birth certificate. The birth certificate was introduced to prove Korematsu's Japanese ancestry, the crucial element in the crime that he was charged with committing.

Fred Korematsu testified on his own behalf. He stated that his parents were born in Japan, but that he had never been there. In fact, he said that he had never left the continental United States. Korematsu testified that he had graduated from Stoner's Grammar School in Oakland and from Castlement High School there. He had attended Los Angeles Junior College in 1938, where he studied chemistry. He had to work after school hours to pay his college expenses, and he, eventually, had to abandon his studies in order to support himself.

After leaving junior college, Fred Korematsu studied welding. He worked as a welder in a Los Angeles shipyard for two and one-half months. After Pearl Harbor, his employer fired him, because he was Japanese.

Korematsu testified that he returned to Oakland to work at his father's nursery and worked there until he left home in April.

Korematsu said that he wanted to fight on behalf of the United States, but that he was rejected because of a stomach ulcer. He registered to vote when he was twenty-one and had never renounced his American citizenship. He testified that he was ready, willing and able to bear arms for the United States:

> "I am willing to enlist. As a citizen of the United States I am ready to render any service that I may be called upon to render to our government in our war against the Axis nations, including the Empire of Japan. I do not owe any allegiance to any country or nation other than the United States of America. I have no dual allegiance. My birth has not, either with my consent or to my knowledge, been registered with any consul of the Empire of Japan. I have never attended and never cared to attend any Japanese school. I am not familiar with the Japanese language . . . . I understand a little Japanese when it is spoken."

The trial was held before Judge St. Sure, without a jury. The judge found Fred Korematsu guilty, but did not fine him, even though the maximum penalty for the offense charged was a fine of $5,000 and/or imprisonment for one year. The judge sentenced Korematsu to five years probation and released him to the custody of the U.S. Army. The Army sent him to the Tanforan

A typical Japanese internment camp, courtesy of the Library of Congress.

Assembly Center, where he joined his family.
Thereafter, he was moved under military guard to the
War Relocation Center in a desolate desert location
near Topaz, Utah.

While his client was confined at Tanforan, Korematsu's attorney, Wayne Collins, appealed the case to
the Ninth Circuit Court of Appeals in San Francisco.
On December 2, 1942, the court issued a terse decision
affirming Korematsu's conviction.

Attorney Collins appealed to the United States
Supreme Court. After briefs were filed, the Supreme
Court heard extensive oral arguments in October, 1944,
at the beginning of the court's term. The arguments
were heard over a two-day period, which is most unusual. During the appellate process, Korematsu was held
without bail for more than two years, even though the
maximum penalty for the "crime" alleged was one
year's imprisonment. In December, 1944, the court issued its ruling.

The Justification

Justice Hugo Black, one of the court's more liberal
jurists, wrote the opinion for the court:

> "We uphold the exclusion order as of the
> time it was made and when petitioner
> [Korematsu] violated it. In doing so we
> are not unmindful of the hardships im-
> posed by it upon a large number of
> American citizens. But hardships are part
> of war, and war is an aggregation of
> hardships."

Justice Black was joined in his opinion by Justices William O. Douglas, Stanley Reed, Chief Justice Harlan Stone and Wiley Rutledge. Justice Felix Frankfurter voted with the majority but wrote a separate opinion. However, Justice Owen Roberts, disagreed, pointing out that:

> "This is not a case of keeping people off the streets at night as was in *Hirabayashi v. United States,* nor a case of temporary exclusion of a citizen from an area for his own safety or that of the community. On the contrary, it is the case of convicting a citizen as a punishment for not submitting to imprisonment in a concentration camp, based on his ancestry, and solely because of his ancestry, without evidence or inquiry concerning his loyalty and good disposition towards the United States."[1]

Justices Frank Murphy and Robert Jackson joined Justice Roberts in his courageous dissent.

Epilogue

The precedent of the *Korematsu* case is alarming. If the United States and Israel were at war with each other, *Korematsu* would give the U.S. government the authority to intern every Jewish American, whether he was a citizen or not. Similarly, if the United States and Mexico were involved in a border war, every Mexican-American could be held in a concentration camp under this nighmarish ruling.

Various proposals have been put forward in Congress to compensate the more than 100,000 Japanese-Americans who were interned during World War II. Of course, monetary compensation cannot adequately replace the years of freedom that the victims lost. However, in order to set the record straight, and to prevent the possibility of such an incident from happening again, Congress ought to act to offer compensation to the Americans of Japanese ancestry who were deprived of their freedom during the war.

Fred Korematsu and other Americans of Japanese ancestry filed a new lawsuit in 1983, alleging that the Justice Department of the Army fabricated the threat caused by Japanese-Americans. The government joined in Korematsu's petition to have his conviction overturned. The judge stated: "as historical precedent it [the 1944 case] stands as a constant caution that in times of war or declared military necessity our institutions must be vigilant in protecting constitutional guarantees." The court noted that the decision was overruled by the court of history, but did not overturn Korematsu's conviction.

Korematsu suffered his entire life because of his conviction. No government agency or large corporation would hire him, because he was convicted of a crime. Korematsu wanted to get a real estate license, but his conviction prevented it. He worked, and continues to work, as a draftsman.

After the war, he moved to Detroit where he met his wife, Kathryn Parsons. Ida Boitano went to Korematsu's parent's nursery after the war to look for him, but has not seen Fred since 1944. She married someone else. In 1949, Korematsu and his wife moved back to California where they raised their family, a son and a daughter. The Korematsus now live in San Leandro, where he is semi-retired at age sixty-eight.

Conclusion

The Supreme Court issued its decision on Monday, December 18, 1944, a day which will live in infamy. While December 7, 1941, as seen in its historical perspective, can be viewed as a day when America slept, and the Japanese took a strategic advantage, the *Korematsu* decision is seen by the entire world as evidence of American discrimination against Orientals, and, as evidence of our racism.

Endnotes

1. *Korematsu v. United States*, 323 U.S. 214 (1944).

Chapter Sixteen

Women's Rights

"No state shall deny . . . any person within its jurisdiction equal protection of the laws."

—Fourteenth Amendment

The much-maligned state of New Jersey was the first state to grant women the right to vote under the Constitution. New Jersey allowed women to vote until 1807. Before the Constitution was enacted, from 1691 until 1780, Massachusetts allowed women property owners to vote.

The woman suffrage movement started to become active after the Civil War. In 1868, an intrepid band of women went to the polls to vote in Vineland, New Jersey. Not much is known about this group except that they inspired Susan B. Anthony into action.

Susan B. Anthony

On November 1, 1872, Susan B. Anthony, following the example of the Vineland group, led fourteen women to register and vote in Rochester, New York. Miss Anthony convinced the inspectors of the registration office that she had a right to vote and they registered her. The two Republican registrars agreed to receive her name while the Democratic official objected. A full report of this scene appeared in the afternoon papers. Because of this publicity, a total of about fifty women registered to vote in Rochester that November.

On November 5th, Susan Anthony and six of the women presented themselves at the polling booth. All of their votes were challenged, but they were all received.

The Rochester newspapers covered these events extensively, the Republican newspaper argued in favor of the women while the Democratic newspaper argued against them. On Thanksgiving day, the fourteen women were informed that they were to be prosecuted by the Federal government, and that the Commissioner wished them to come to his office. The ladies refused the invitation.

On the afternoon of Thanksgiving day, Miss Anthony was summoned to her parlor to receive a visitor. He stated, "The Commissioner wishes to arrest you."

Miss Anthony responded, "Is this your usual method of serving a warrant?"

The Marshal gathered his courage, handed her a summons and meekly escorted her to the Commissioner's office. Anthony was arrested for her part in the Rochester incident. In addition, the male election inspectors who registered Anthony and the other females were arrested for registering the women to vote. Inspectors Hall, Marsh and others were tried and convicted in June, 1873, and fined twenty-five dollars. When they refused to pay the fine, they were jailed. During their short jail terms, the ladies of the Eighth Ward brought home-cooked meals to them. President Grant pardoned the inspectors after they had spent a week in jail.

On June 18, 1873, Susan B. Anthony was tried and pronounced guilty of illegally registering and voting by a hostile judge, Ward Hunt, who took the case away from the jury.[1] He said:

> "The Fourteenth Amendment gives no right to a woman to vote, and the voting by Miss Anthony was a violation of the law.
>
> If she believed she had a right to vote, and voted in reliance upon that belief, does that relieve her from the penalty?
>
>   *   *   *
>
> Miss Anthony knew that she was a woman, and that the Constitution of this State prohibits her from voting. She intended to violate that provision—intend-

ed to test it, perhaps, but certainly to
violate it, and this she is presumed to
have intended."

Even though a judge can never direct a verdict
against a defendant in a criminal case, Judge Hunt did
so. He fined Miss Anthony one hundred dollars. Susan
B. Anthony stated:

"May it please your honor, I shall never
pay a dollar of your unjust penalty. All
the stock in trade I possess is a $10,000
debt incurred by publishing my paper—*The Revolution*—the sole object of
which was to educate all women to do
precisely as I have done, rebel against
man-made unjust, unconstitutional forms
of law that tax, fine, imprison and hang
women, while they deny them the right
of representation in the government."

Anthony never paid the fine. Her conviction could
not be appealed because no steps were taken to enforce her sentence. She was unable, as she had hoped,
to appeal her case to the United States Supreme Court.
Other women were getting active in the suffrage movement. One of them was Virginia Minor.

Virginia L. Minor

Virginia L. Minor was a Civil War relief worker.
She married Francis Minor in Virginia when she was
nineteen. He had graduated from Princeton and the
University of Virginia Law School.

Despite their Virginia roots, the Minors supported the Union in the Civil War. Mrs. Minor joined the St. Louis Ladies Union Aid Society, which was organized in 1861 to assist wounded soldiers and their families. When the society was disbanded in 1865, Mrs. Minor and several other women turned their attention to their own rights. She said that not only Negroes but also women should be given the right to vote. She was the first woman in Missouri to take a stand for suffrage.

In 1867, Mrs. Minor circulated a petition to the state legislature that the amendment to the Missouri Constitution permitting male Negroes to vote be extended to women. Her proposed amendment was rejected by a vote of eighty-nine to five. After that, she organized the Women's Suffrage Association of Missouri and was elected president.

Francis Minor, a lawyer, believed that the U.S. Constitution granted women the right to vote. The Constitution does not mention the words male or female, only citizens and persons of the United States. The courts had held that women were citizens, were allowed to own property and were required to pay taxes. Mr. Minor felt that state laws prohibiting women from voting were "bills of attainder." Bills of attainder are laws directed at specific individuals or groups and are outlawed by the Constitution. He also believed that the "privileges and immunities" clause of the Constitution applied to men and women alike. That clause provides that "the citizens of each state shall be entitled to all privileges and immunities of citizens in the several states." But his best argument was that the newly enacted Fourteenth Amendment gave women the right to vote. That amendment provides:

"No State shall make or enforce any law
which shall abridge the privileges or immunities of citizens of the United States .
. . ; nor deny to any person within its
jurisdiction the equal protection of her
laws."

The Challenge

The first step in a legal challenge to Missouri's
"male only" voting was to attempt to register to vote.
On October 15, 1872, Virginia L. Minor, age forty-six,
went to the office of voter registration at 2004 Market
Street in St. Louis, Missouri. The registrar, Reese Happersett, refused to register her to vote. Mr. Happersett
said that she was not entitled to vote because she was
not a male citizen, but a woman. He relied on the then
recently approved Missouri Constitution which declared
that only male citizens were permitted to vote.

The law of Missouri did not allow women to file
suit unless their husbands agreed to join in and support
their case. Mrs. Minor's husband, Francis Minor, agreed
with and encouraged his wife's legal tactics. Francis
Minor and two other male attorneys (a few years
earlier, the Supreme Court had ruled in *Bradwell v.
State*[2] that women had no right to practice law) drafted a lawsuit against Mr. Happersett. Mrs. Minor sued
for $10,000 as damages for deprivation of her right to
vote.

Virginia L. Minor, courtesy of the Library of Congress.

The Missouri Supreme Court made its decision on August 16, 1873. The court ruled that the Missouri law allowing only men to vote was not a bill of attainder. It further ruled that the provision did not run afoul of the privileges and immunities clause. The court said that the continued denial of a right is the fact that everyone has denied it before. The court considered Minor's Fourteenth Amendment argument to be more substantial. However, the court ruled that the intent of the Fourteenth Amendment was to give former slaves the right to vote and not to give women the right to vote.

A fundamental principle of law is that if a provision is clear on its face, there is no need to seek the intent of the drafters. The Fourteenth Amendment is clear on its face that all citizens are to be treated equally.

Woman Suffrage at the Supreme Court

The U.S. Supreme Court agreed to hear Mrs. Minor's appeal. Its decision came on March 29, 1875.[3] The Supreme Court of the United States was unanimous in its ruling:

> "There is no doubt that women may be citizens.
>
> *   *   *
>
> For nearly ninety years the people have acted upon the idea that the Constitution, when it conferred citizenship, did not necessarily confer the right of suffrage."

The all-male Supreme Court voted that women had no right to vote, as they had ruled that women had no right to practice law. Women's rights were left in the hands of men.

Epilogue

The year after the Supreme Court's ruling in Mrs. Minor's case, the country celebrated its one hundredth anniversary. There was a centennial celebration in Philadelphia where Susan B. Anthony proclaimed a Women's Declaration of Rights. In 1877, Ms. Anthony led a group of women onto the floor of the United States Senate, bearing suffrage petitions. The Senate, after making the standard jokes concerning women's status as property, referred the petition to the Committee on Public Lands.

In the following year Senator Aaron Sargent of California introduced a constitutional amendment:

> "The right of citizens of the United States to vote shall not be denied or abridged by the United States or any State on account of sex."

In 1886, the Senate voted the amendment down by a margin of thirty-four to six, with thirty-two senators not voting. In 1890, the State of Wyoming became the only state to allow women to vote. Colorado followed in 1893, Utah in 1895 and Idaho the following year. Washington State and California followed in 1910 and 1911. Kansas, Oregon and Arizona approved women's suffrage in 1912, Nevada and Montana in 1914. The only eastern state to join the trend was New York in 1917.

Forty-one years after being introduced by Senator Sargent, the Nineteenth Amendment was approved. Thirty-six states ratified the women's rights amendment, and it became a part of the Constitution on August 26, 1920.

During the 1980s, more than one hundred years after the Supreme Court's ruling in Mrs. Minor's case, the Equal Rights Amendment failed to become a part of the Constitution. The ERA is still needed because, at any given time, the male-dominated Supreme Court can refuse to give women equal protection of the law, as they did in 1875.

Endnotes

1. *United States v. Anthony*, Case No. 14,459, 24 Fed. Case 829 (1873).
2. 16 Wall. 130 (1872).
3. *Minor v. Happersett*, 21 Wallace 162 (1875).

PART 5
Criminal Rights

Chapter Seventeen

The Right to an Attorney

"In all criminal prosecutions, the accused shall . . . have the assistance of counsel for his defence."

—Sixth Amendment.

Smith Betts was an unemployed thirty-six-year-old farm worker who was on welfare back in 1938. He lived in Hagerstown in rural western Maryland. In the summer, the Maryland hills are covered with acres of corn and other crops, and when Smitty worked, he cut corn or performed other farm duties. But the economy was still in the midst of the Depression, and there isn't much farm work in the winter.

Mr. Betts had lived with Mary Emerson for three years, and she was considered his wife. On the day before Christmas of 1938, Smitty got his welfare check from the Washington County Welfare Fund for ten dollars. Betts paid his landlord, George Uhler, five dollars toward his rent.

Christmas Eve Robbery

Norman Bollinger was a teenager who worked at the Medford Grocery Store, a small rural store in the rolling hills of Carroll County. It was dark when Bollinger closed the store at 5:00 p.m. on Christmas Eve, 1938. A few minutes after closing, he walked to his car. An old green Chevrolet with red wheels pulled up and slowed down. Bollinger thought it was a last-minute customer. A man, dressed in a dark overcoat, dark amber glasses and a hat, with a handkerchief over his chin, got out of the car.

The man said to the teenaged Bollinger: "Hey, buddy, what do you have there?" He then asked for the bag, which contained twenty-four dollars in bills and twenty-six dollars worth of coins. Bollinger said, "Like fun." The man pulled a gun from his coat pocket, and Bollinger gave him the bag. Bollinger failed to get the license number of the car but phoned ahead to alert others down the highway of the robbery and immediately ran to tell the store owner what had happened.

The Senator and the Sheriff

The Medford County Grocery Store was owned by State Senator J. David Baile. When Bollinger told him about the robbery, Baile called Sheriff Walter Shipley, who began an investigation. His investigation led to Smith Betts, whom people in Medford reported seeing in the vicinity of the Medford County Store. Senator Baile placed an advertisement in the Westminster newspaper:

$50 REWARD

for information leading to arrest of two men who held up our Clerk, Norman Bollinger, at 5:05 o'clock, Saturday evening at Branch Store.

The man who leveled the gun on Norman and demanded the change bag of $24.00 in silver and $26.00 in paper money was about 35-years-old, 200 pounds and 6 feet tall.

They left in a 1930 Chevrolet Coach with red-disc-orange wheels. If you happened to be passing the branch at 5 minutes after 5 perhaps you can help identify this car.

Several days after the robbery, Bollinger was called to the jail where the State Police had Smith Betts in custody. Norman Bollinger said that he could not identify Betts as the thief. At Bollinger's request, the police put glasses and a handkerchief on Betts' face. After that, Bollinger said that Betts was the robber.

The Trial

Smitty Betts was arraigned at the Carroll County Circuit Court. He was charged with armed robbery, an offense which had a maximum penalty of over ten years.

Smith Betts had had an earlier run-in with the law. He had pleaded guilty to larceny (theft without a weapon) and served a short sentence.

This time Mr. Betts pleaded not guilty. He asked Judge William H. Forsythe to appoint an attorney to represent him because he was poor, on welfare and could not afford to pay an attorney. The judge said that the usual practice was to appoint attorneys to poor defendants who were charged with murder, man-slaughter or rape. The judge refused Betts' request and said that he would have to defend himself.

The State called Norman Bollinger as a witness, and he identified Smitty as the gunman. Other witnesses were called to show that Smith Betts was in the vicinity of the crime within a day or two of the robbery.

Betts called six witnesses who stated that he was in his apartment all day when the robbery was took place. His landlord testified that he saw him several times during the day. The landlord's wife confirmed Betts' alibi, as did a neighbor and his common law wife, Mary.

Officer B.C. Mason of the Maryland State Police testified. He said he learned that Smith Betts was in the vicinity of the store Thursday, December 22, two days before the robbery, with another fellow Ells Dunn. Dunn owned a 1928 Chevrolet with a blue body and black fenders. Betts did not own a car.

Smith Betts did not testify on his own behalf. The judge found Betts guilty as charged and sentenced him to eight years in the Maryland House of Corrections.

Habeas Corpus

After spending two years in jail, convinced that he was innocent and that he did not get a fair trial, Betts prepared and filed a petition for *habeas corpus*. Smith

Betts was not an educated man, but he learned a fair amount about law while he was incarcerated. *Habeas corpus*, means "you must have the body." *A habeas corpus* petition is a document filed by, or on behalf of, a prisoner, who claims that he is wrongfully detained in custody. Betts still was not represented by an attorney.

Judge Joseph Mish, in Hagerstown, granted Betts' writ on June 5, 1941, and ordered a hearing for June 17. After the hearing, Mish returned Betts to the Maryland Penitentiary.

A few months later, Betts filed a new petition for a writ of *habeas corpus* with Judge Carroll Bond, the chief judge of Maryland's highest court. This time, an attorney, Jesse Slingluff of Baltimore, represented Mr. Betts. Slingluff was paid by an organization who wanted a test case to challenge the denial of counsel to poor defendants. Judge Bond denied Betts relief, because he believed that Betts had a fair trial and did a reasonably good job of defending himself.

Slingluff then applied to the United States Supreme Court to appeal Judge Bond's decision. The Supreme Court accepted the case.

In the Supreme Court

Attorney Slingluff argued that the Sixth Amendment requires that counsel be appointed to those accused of serious crimes when they cannot afford their own lawyer.

By a vote of six to three, the Supreme Court ruled that Betts did not have the right to have an attorney appointed to represent him.[1] Justice Owen Roberts wrote the court's opinion. He ruled that while those accused of federal crimes have the right to have counsel appointed, those accused of state crimes do not.

While some of the amendments to the Constitution specifically apply (at least on their face) to the federal government, the Sixth Amendment does not. The Sixth Amendment begins "in *all* criminal prosecutions the accused shall . . . ." According to the amendment, accused persons have the right to a speedy and public trial, the right to confront witnesses, the right to a jury trial and the right to have the assistance of counsel.

The court could have justified its decision by saying that nothing requires the State of Maryland to pay an attorney to represent every individual charged with a crime. But the Supreme Court, without foundation in the Constitution, ruled that those accused of state crimes did not have the right to have attorneys represent them.

Epilogue

Smith Betts served out his sentence. Twenty-one years later, the same issue again came before the Supreme Court. In one of the few cases in which the court specifically overruled an earlier decision, the landmark decision of *Gideon v. Wainwright*[2] overturned the *Betts* case. The new decision was approved by all nine members of the court. All of the six members of the majority in the *Betts* decision retired from the court, while two of the three dissenters (Black and Douglas) joined the new majority. A book and a movie about Gideon's case, both called *Gideon's Trumpet*, were produced in the 1960s.

The Shipley name is common in the Carroll County. In 1987, the Clerk of the Court is named Shipley, and other Shipleys are employed in the courthouse. During the same week as the 1938 Medford robbery, the sheriff's son, Russell Shipley, was arrested for stealing $3000 in a break-in. Russell Shipley was sentenced to three years in jail for breaking and entering. He got the best legal representation that money could buy. On the other hand, Smitty Betts was charged with stealing only fifty dollars, but was sentenced to eight years in prison. If Betts had had an attorney, he would have demanded a jury trial and probably would have been acquitted. Unfortunately, he got all the justice that he could afford.

Endnotes

1. 316 U.S. 455 (1942).
2. 372 U.S. 335 (1963).

Chapter Eighteen

Cruel and Unusual Punishment

"My object all sublime
I shall achieve in time—
To make the punishment fit the crime."

—Gilbert & Sullivan
The Lord High Executioner
The Mikado

William James "Scotty" Rummel hung around with the wrong kind of friends. When he was sixteen, he stole a case of beer. A year later, along with a buddy, he broke into a Western Auto store in Karnes City, Texas.

Rummel was born in 1942 and reared by his grandparents in Karnes City. He dropped out of high school to do construction work and odd jobs in San Antonio. There wasn't a lot of work to go around, so he did what he had to do.

He is six feet tall, blond and weighs two-hundred pounds. His life has not been easy. Rummel has been divorced three times. His body is marked by numerous scars and tattoos.

In 1964, at the age of twenty-two, Bill Rummel's well-worn Studebaker badly needed new tires. An acquaintance gave him a credit card, and he charged eighty dollars worth of tires at Harvey Helton's Enco gasoline station in San Antonio. The credit card was a stolen card. Rummel claims that he didn't know the card was stolen but admitted that he had a pretty good idea that it was hot. He pleaded guilty, was sentenced to three years in prison, but was released after twenty months incarceration. It was his first felony conviction.

Rummel was released in 1966 and spent the next three years working on a series of construction and repair jobs. In 1969, at the age of twenty-seven Bill Rummel was living in the Angeles Motel in San Antonio. His rent of $28.36 was due weekly. He was having problems paying his bills and had been threatened with eviction. To keep a roof over his head, he forged a check for $28.36. Again Rummel pleaded guilty. Rummel was sentenced to spend another four years with the Texas Department of Corrections. Rummel was released in 1971 after serving a year and a half. This was his second felony conviction.

In the Heat of San Antonio

On a blazing hot day in August, 1972, Rummel walked into Captain Hook's Lounge in San Antonio. In the bar, he recognized Paul Ellis and headed for the door, but Ellis caught him. "Hey Scotty, come over here." Rummel owed Ellis twenty dollars, and Ellis demanded his money. Bill Rummel had a ten dollar bill and some change in his pockets and handed Ellis the ten.

Rummel stuck around and watched men playing pool. He overheard Ellis talking to David Shaw, owner of the bar, about getting his air conditioner fixed. Rummel had worked for Mike's Air Conditioning Service and offered his services to repair the air conditioning unit.

The air conditioner needed a new compressor. Rummel called Service Supply, a parts wholesaler, for the price of a replacement compressor and was told $120.75. Ellis, not trusting "Scotty," advised Shaw to write a check to Service Supply. Rummel took the check.

Service Supply wouldn't sell the compressor to Rummel, because he wasn't an authorized dealer. Rummel went to a drive-in teller at Shaw's bank and cashed the check, signing his name and Service Supply. Rummel claims that he intended to buy a compressor from Montgomery Ward, but it cost more than from Service Supply. Rummel had no extra money of his own, so he tried to reach Shaw at Captain Hook's Lounge.

Bill Rummel was not the most reliable repairman around. On occasion, he would remember his promise to repair the air conditioner, but he never got around to it. It turned out to be the biggest mistake that he made in his life.

In September, Shaw filed a complaint with the
police concerning Rummel's theft of the $120.75.
Rummel was picked up by the police on a charge of
"theft of over $50 by false pretext," concerning the
$120.75 he pocketed for the air conditioner repair.
William B. Chenault III was appointed by the court to
represent Rummel. Chenault said that "he didn't think
that it was the duty of a court-appointed lawyer to go
out into a bunch of sleazy bars on the bad side of
town and look for witnesses . . . I wasn't about to go
there for the $250 I was being paid for this case."

The Trial

On the day of trial, April 10, 1973, Rummel's
attorney asked to withdraw from the case. The court
denied the request. During the trial, Chenault called no
witnesses on Rummel's behalf and advised Rummel not
to testify.

Two days before trial, Rummel's parents paid Mr.
Shaw fifty dollars towards the loss he had incurred
when dealing with their son. Shaw signed a non-
prosecution agreement in exchange for this payment.
But the court refused to admit the document into evidence, because it had no bearing on his innocence or
guilt. The jury never got a chance to see it.

The trial lasted two days. The government subpoe-
naed Shaw to testify and called two tellers from the
bank to verify that Rummel had cashed the check. Another witness testified that Rummel had never worked
for the Service Supply company. Hearsay testimony
(testimony given by someone who was not a direct

witness) was given to the effect that Rummel had been to Service Supply to discuss purchase of the compressor. The court disallowed the testimony because hearsay testimony is generally not admissable in court.

The jury made their decision quickly. Primarily, because Rummel did not testify on his own behalf, the jury convicted him of his third felony, theft by pretext.

The Three-Time Loser Law

The law in Texas provided that once a person is convicted of three felonies, regardless of the severity of the offense, the judge must sentence the "three-time loser" to life imprisonment. Judge John Benavides followed the law, and William James "Scotty" Rummel was sentenced to life with the Texas Department of Corrections.

The Jailhouse Lawyer

Bill Rummel is much smarter than one would guess. Although he never graduated from high school, in prison he became a scholar. Rummel started reading legal books and court decisions, randomly, not certain where to begin. He read through hundreds of legal books in the prison law library at the Texas Department of Corrections' Retrieve Unit, near Angleton, Texas, and became adept at filing legal briefs.

At first, his legal appeals were rejected. He filed a two-page writ for appeal, in 1975, with the state court of criminal appeals. The court rejected this petition, so he filed a forty-five page brief with the U.S. District

Court. This court, too, rejected his petitions, appeals and motions. Then the Fifth Circuit Court of Appeals, the federal appeals court for most of the southeastern United States granted him a hearing. This appellate court appointed a young lawyer, Scott Atlas, to represent him. Atlas had recently finished a clerkship with one of the judges on the court and had begun working for the prestigious Houston law firm of Vinson & Elkins.

On Atlas' Shoulders

Scott Atlas knew that he was appointed to a potentially precedent-setting case. He argued that the life sentence given to his client was cruel and unusual punishment, which is prohibited by the Eighth Amendment to the Constitution.

In New Orleans in March, 1978, Atlas won a favorable ruling from a divided three-judge panel of the court of appeals.[1] The court ruled that the life sentence "was so grossly disproportionate" to his offenses that it could constitute cruel and unusual punishment.

The State of Texas was not about to take this setback lying down. The attorney general's office in Texas filed an unusual request for the entire Fifth Circuit court to rehear the case, all fourteen judges sitting at once.

The court granted the request, which is normally a hundred to one shot. In December of 1978, by a vote of eight to four, the full court of appeals reversed Rummel's victory.[2]

The Court of Last Resort

Atlas filed the necessary papers, and the Supreme Court agreed to hear the case. The case was set for argument in January of 1980.

On March 18, 1980, in a five to four decision, the court ruled that Rummel's sentence was not a cruel or unusual punishment.[3] Justice Rehnquist wrote the opinion for the court, explaining that life imprisonment for a traffic offense would be cruel and unusual punishment but that Rummel's crimes were serious, and that he would not overturn the law of the State of Texas imprisoning him for life.

Justice Powell, joined by Justices Brennan, Marshall and Stevens, dissented, arguing that Rummel's crimes were non-violent:

> "It is difficult to imagine felonies that pose less danger to the peace and good order of society than the three crimes committed by the petitioner."

Rummel's third offense, the one that caused him to be sentenced to life in prison was barely a criminal offense at all. Thousands of times every day, repair shops take money for repairs that are not made, or are made ineffectively. That is, in essence, what Bill Rummel was convicted of. He was given money (the check for the part) to make an air conditioner repair, and he failed to make the repair. It is the type of offense that is usually handled as a civil claim in small claims court and is *not* unlike a minor traffic offense. In fact, a minor traffic offense can be more serious because speeding or reckless driving can cause injury or death, and Rummel only caused a small economic loss.

While it is true that Rummel committed an act of poor judgment when he cashed the check, many a driver also uses poor judgment when he gets behind the wheel while intoxicated. But, the State of Texas considers this offense a misdemeanor the first time it is committed.

Epilogue

In 1983, the State of Texas amended its "three-time loser" law, deleting its mandatory life sentence provision. Also in 1983, the Supreme Court overturned the *Rummel* precedent and ruled that a life sentence for a series of minor crimes does constitute cruel and unusual punishment.[4] Justice Harry Blackmun apparently changed his mind and made up part of the new five to four majority. Justice Powell wrote the new opinion.

William James Rummel won his release from the Texas prison system on other grounds. After defeat in the Supreme Court, his attorney went back into court and successfully argued that Rummel's first attorney provided him with an ineffective defense. After spending seven years, nine months and fifteen days of his life sentence William Rummel left prison as a free man.

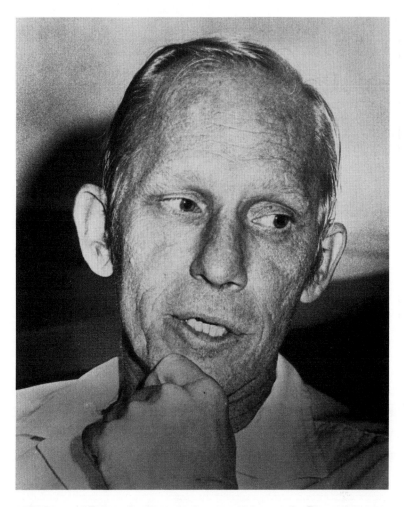

William "Scotty" Rummel, courtesy of San Antonio Light.

Endnotes

1. 568 F.2d 1193 (1978)
2. 587 F.2d 651 (1979)
3. 445 U.S. 263 (1980)
4. *Solem v. Helm,* No. 82-492, 51 L.W. 5019.

Chapter Nineteen

The Presumption of Innocence

"You don't have many suspects innocent of a crime."

—Attorney General Edwin Meese

Our criminal justice system, based on the Constitution, has always presumed those charged with crimes to be innocent until proven guilty. The Eighth Amendment provides that "Excessive bail shall not be required . . ." For 200 years, our courts have allowed persons charged with crimes to be set free on bail or on their personal recognizance.

There is an expression used by lawyers which is fitting here: "bad facts make for bad law." The individuals involved in the case described in this chapter are not very appealing.

Fat Tony and Friends

Anthony "Fat Tony" Salerno was the "boss" of the
Genovese Family of La Cosa Nostra, the Mafia. Vin-
cent "Fish" Cafaro was a captain in the organization. In
1986, Salerno and Cafaro were arrested after being
charged in a twenty-nine-count indictment alleging ex-
tortion, mail fraud, gambling violations and conspiracy
to commit murder. The government sought to have Salerno and Cafaro detained in jail on the grounds that
no condition of release could assure the safety of the
community. The goverment claimed that Salerno had
participated in two murder conspiracies.

Salerno was then seventy-four and suffering from
high blood pressure, complicated by congestive heart
failure since 1961. In 1981, Salerno suffered from a
stroke from which he had recovered with some limited
residual disability.

In the Lower Courts

Salerno and Cafaro were arrested on March 21, 1986.
They were incarcerated without bail. At their arraign-
ment a week later, the government moved for their
"pre-trial detention." The federal government contended
that because the defendants represented a danger to
society, they should be held in jail, without bail, until
after trial. Judge John Walker, Jr. agreed with the
prosecutor that Salerno could order a murder merely
by voicing his assent and ordered both defendants held
in preventive detention until trial.[1]

The district court granted the government's motion

for preventive detention, and ordered Salerno and Cafaro to jail pending trial. Judge Walker stated:

"The activities of a criminal organization such as the Genovese Family do not cease with the arrest of its principals and their release even on the most stringent of bail conditions. The illegal businesses, in place for many years, require constant attention and protection, or they will fail. Under these circumstances, this court recognizes a strong incentive on the part of its leadership to continue business as usual. When business as usual involves threats, beatings, and murder, the present danger such people pose in the community is self-evident."

It was never mentioned that even while in jail, Salerno could order someone to be murdered.

Salerno and Cafaro appealed. The United States Court of Appeals sitting in New York took the case up promptly and issued its opinion in July.[2]

By a vote of two to one, the court of appeals reversed the order of preventive detention. The court ruled that the Bail Reform Act, passed in 1984, which authorized preventive detention, was unconstitutional, because the detention order was based on the likelihood of Salerno and Cafaro committing crimes in the future. Judge Kearse, of the court of appeals, stated that preventive detention to prevent future crimes is

"repugnant to the concept of substantive

due process, which we believe prohibits
the total deprivation of liberty."

The court of appeals ruling freed Anthony Salerno,
as well as Cafaro, from prison. The government appealed to the United States Supreme Court.

"Fish" Gets Off the Hook

In early October 1986, Cafaro became a cooperating
witness for the government, and the government agreed
to let him post a personal recognizance bond of one
million dollars for his continued freedom. Apparently,
the government felt that once Cafaro agreed to cooperate, his threat to society vanished. This was what happened, but this was not what Salerno or the Supreme
Court justices, then determining whether they would
hear the case, were told. The Solicitor General told the
court that Cafaro was "temporarily released for medical
treatment." As Justice Marshall later wrote, "I do not
understand how the Solicitor General's representation
that Cafaro was 'still subject to the pretrial detention
order' can be reconciled with the fact of his release on
a $1,000,000 personal recognizance bond."

Fat Tony Avoids the Slammer

Not long afterward, on November 19, 1986, Salerno
was convicted of other federal charges, and, on January
13, 1987, he was sentenced to one hundred years' imprisonment. With the agreement of the federal govern-

Anthony "Fat Tony" Salerno, courtesy of New York Daily News.

ment, Salerno not jailed, pending appeal, apparently in order to keep Salerno's other case alive before the Supreme Court. The Justice Department wanted to take the issue of pretrial detention before the Supreme Court, and they wanted to do so in a case involving a very undesirable, even despicable defendant. Salerno fit the part perfectly.

At the Supreme Court

The Supreme Court agreed to hear the appeal. On May 26, 1987, the court, by a vote of six to three, handed down its decision. The nation's highest court reversed the decision once again and upheld the preventive detention law.[3]

Justice William Rehnquist, a former Justice Department official, wrote the opinion for the court. He contended that pretrial detention is not punishment; it is a "regulatory" procedure. Rehnquist states: "the mere fact that a person is detained does not inexorably lead to the conclusion that the government has imposed punishment." He is playing a semantic game with the Constitution which can lead to no long-term good. Under Rehnquist's view of the Constitution, the judge is not finding the defendant guilty of anything, but is acting as a regulatory agency. Much as the Federal Aviation Administration regulates air travel to protect air commuters, the judge regulates the defendant's conduct by ordering him detained to protect the public. Rehnquist quotes the constitutional ban on deprivation of liberty without due process, but explains how a man can be deprived of liberty without a jury finding him guilty. However, whether he is held due to a regulatory finding or a jury verdict does not matter to the defendant locked in jail.

Justice Thurgood Marshall, joined by Justice William Brennan in dissent, stated:

> "Honoring the presumption of innocence is often difficult; sometimes we must pay substantial social costs as a result of our commitment to the values we espouse. But at the end of the day the presumption of innocence protects the innocent; the shortcuts we take with those whom we believe to be guilty injure only those wrongfully accused and, ultimately, ourselves.
>
> Throughout the world today there are men, women, and children interned indefinitely, awaiting trials which may never come or which may be a mockery of the world, because their governments believe them to be "dangerous." Our Constitution, whose construction began two centuries ago, can shelter us forever from the evils of such unchecked power. Over two hundred years it has slowly, through our efforts, grown more durable, more expansive, and more just. But it cannot protect us if we lack the courage, and the self-restraint, to protect ourselves. Today a majority of the Court applies itself to an ominous exercise in demolition. Theirs is truly a decision which will go forth without authority, and come back without respect."

Justice John Paul Stevens wrote a separate dissenting opinion. He felt that in some case in the future it might be appropriate to detain someone who had not committed a crime. Justice Stevens gave the example of a demented hijacker who was found innocent because of his insanity. However, we would commit such a man under a commitment proceeding, an emergency one if necessary, and not under the preventive detention provision of the Bail Reform Act.

Epilogue

Today, thousands of Americans charged with federal crimes are held in preventive detention. Some of them may be found guilty. Many probably will not. All should be presumed innocent until proven guilty, as those charged with crimes in America have been for 200 years.

Mr. Salerno is now in federal detention in New York and is likely to remain so for the rest of his life. Added to his crimes is his destruction of the presumption of innocence in the United States.

Endnotes

1. 631 F.Supp. 1364 (1986).
2. 794 F.2d 64 (1986).
3. 481 U.S. 739 (1987).

PART 6
Access to Justice

Chapter Twenty

Storming the Castle

"The house of every one is to him as his castle and fortress, as well for his defence against injury and violence as for his repose."

—Sir Edward Coke, *Semayne's Case*

"The right of the people to be secure in persons, houses, papers . . . against unreasonable searches . . . shall not be violated . . . ."

— Fourth Amendment

It was a quiet Friday evening in St. Paul, Minnesota in November of 1983. The Creighton family, Robert and Sarisse, and their two young daughters, Shaunda and Tiffany, were watching television. Their home was on West Minnehaha Street, within a mile and a half of the Capitol dome. It was calm; Mrs. Creighton fell asleep.

Robert Creighton worked in the stockroom for the telephone company. Mrs. Creighton worked in the chancellors office of the state university system. The Creighton family could be characterized as a hard-working, middle-class, black family.

A Light in the Window

Near the end of the television show, *Webster*, a bright spotlight suddenly flashed through the Creighton front window. Mr. Creighton opened the door and was confronted with about seven police officers and an FBI agent, many of them brandishing shotguns. All of them were white.

One of the officers told Creighton "to keep his hands in sight" while the others rushed through the front door. Creighton asked if they had a search warrant and one of them told him, "We don't have a search warrant and don't need one; you watch too much TV."

Robert Creighton told the men to put their guns away because they were frightening the children, but they refused. Sarisse Creighton awoke to the shrieking of her children and was confronted by an officer who pointed a shotgun at her. She overheard an officer yelling at her daughters to "sit their damn asses down and stop screaming." Mrs. Creighton asked the officer, "What the hell is going on?"

The officer did not explain the situation and simply said to her, "Why don't you make your damn kids sit on the couch and make them shut up?"

One officer asked Mr. Creighton if he owned a red
and silver Buick Riviera. He said that he owned a
maroon Oldsmobile. As Creighton led the officers
downstairs to his garage, one of the officers punched
him in the face, knocking him to the ground and
causing him to bleed from his mouth and forehead.
Creighton was attempting to move past the officer to
open the garage door, when the officer panicked and
hit him. The officer claimed that he thought Creighton
was attempting to grab his shotgun, even though
Creighton was not a suspect in any crime and had no
contraband in his house. Shaunda, the Creightons'
ten-year-old daughter, witnessed her father being as-
saulted and screamed for her mother to help. One of
the officers then hit her.

Sarisse Creighton telephoned her mother, but an
officer kicked and grabbed the phone and told her to
"hang up that damn phone." She told her children to
run to their neighbor's house for safety.

The children ran out and a plainclothes officer ran
after them. The officer ran into the neighbor's home
and grabbed Shaunda by the shoulders and shook her
violently. The neighbor told the officer, "Can't you see
she's in shock? Leave her alone and get out of my
house." Mrs. Creigton's mother later brought Shaunda
to the emergency room at Children's Hospital for an
arm injury caused by the officer's rough handling of
her.

During the melee, family members and friends began arriving at the Creighton home. Sarisse Creighton
asked FBI agent Russell Anderson if he had a search
warrant. He replied, "I don't need a damn search

warrant when I'm looking for a fugitive."

At about 3:30 in the afternoon, there was a robbery in St. Paul, which allegedly was perpetrated by Vadaain Dixon, Mrs. Creighton's brother. Before searching the Creighton's home, the police had searched the homes of Dixon's mother and grandmother, also without a search warrant.

Anderson claimed that he had probable cause to search the homes of Dixon's relatives and that it would have been too difficult to get a search warrant. He believed that "exigent circumstances" justified the searches.

Violating Fourth Amendment Rights

The Creightons were badly shaken, embarrassed, and two of them were physically injured. They consulted John Sheehy, a Minneapolis lawyer across the Mississippi River, from their home. Sheehy explained to them that the Fourth Amendment to the Constitution requires that police get search warrants before conducting a search of anyone's home. The only exception to the law, he explained, is when the police are in "hot pursuit" of a criminal, for example, a high-speed chase from the scene of a crime.

Attorney Sheehy filed suit on behalf of the Creightons for deprivation of their civil rights under the Constitution, for assault and battery, false arrest and false imprisonment.

In Federal Court

The government attorneys moved to dismiss the case, claiming that the police officers could not be sued because they believed that what they were doing was lawful. The District Court Judge Diana Murphy dismissed the Creighton's lawsuit.

The Creighton's attorney filed an appeal. The court of appeals reversed the lower court's ruling.[1] Judge Heaney ruled:

> "A mere suspicion that a suspect *might* be in the home of a third party generally will not establish probable cause to search the third party's home.

> * * *

> Clearly, such speculation is not a reasonable ground justifying the invasion of citizens' privacy."

The court of appeals also found that the district court erred by finding that the police were in "hot pursuit," and ruled that as a matter of law there was no hot pursuit because there was no chase or continuous hunt. Judge Heaney further stated that the search was illegal and sent the case back to Judge Murphy for a trial.

The Supreme Court

The government attorneys were not at all pleased

with the prospect of an FBI agent and seven police officers as defendants in a trial for damages. They attempted a longshot: an appeal to the Supreme Court
before the case went back to the district court for trial.

The Supreme Court took the unusual step of accept-
ing a case that did not have a developed record. There
had been no trial, only a decision by the district court
on a motion.

The justices voted in conference and split six to
three. The case was assigned to Justice Scalia, a recent
appointee to the court. He said "It is not possible . . .
to say that one 'reasonably' acted unreasonably." Since
the Fourth Amendment protects citizens against "unreasonable" searches, a finding that the officer was not
reasonable should mean that the search was illegal. But
Justice Scalia, although he admitted that the search was
illegal, found a way to find police officers and FBI
agents immune from suits even when they have violated the Fourth Amendment. He twisted the language
of the Fourth Amendment, claiming that its was
unfortunate. Scalia believed that the Fourth Amendment should protect citizens against "undue searches"
and not "unreasonable" ones. Justice Scalia's opinion
was announced on June 25, 1987.

Justices Stevens, Brennan and Marshall dissented.
Justice Stevens asserted that the majority:

> "announces a new rule of law that
> protects federal agents who make forcible
> nighttime entries into the homes of
> innocent citizens without probable cause,
> without a warrant, and without any valid

reason for their warrantless search. The Court stunningly restricts the constitutional accountability of the police . . . by displaying remarkably little fidelity to the countervailing principles of individual liberty and privacy that infuse the Fourth Amendment.

Epilogue

The *Creighton* case was handed down just before this book went to press. I have used it in place of another Fourth Amendment case that was not quite as egregious. However, the Supreme Court has been undercutting the Fourth Amendment in many recent decisions. Fourth Amendment rights have been limited in trailer homes, in barns and in back yards. The Supreme Court has recently ruled that the police, without a warrant, are allowed to search your property from airplanes and helicopters.

As Justice Rehnquist stated, these cases might well "surprise or even shock those who lived in an earlier era." His statement was made when announcing that the Bank Secrecy Act was constitutional, even though it required banks, without warrants or probable cause, to supply the IRS and other government agencies bank records of customers. In that 1974 decision, Justice Douglas dissented, opposing the "sledge-hammer approach" of the law and the underlying assumption that "every citizen is a crook."

The problem, now, is that the Supreme Court is allowing the police to act as if every citizen is a criminal. The rights of innocent citizens were trampled by the gestapo-like actions of the St. Paul Police Department and the FBI in Minnesota, on Veterans' Day in 1983, and the nation's highest court has given its seal of approval. The Fourth Amendment's requirement of a warrant, etched in the Constitution, is now as meaningless as an epitaph etched on a tombstone, with no one left to enforce it.

Endnotes

1. 766 F.2d 1269 (1985).

Chapter Twenty-One

Indecent Exposure

"In any country there must be people who have to die. They are the sacrifices any nation has to make."

—Idi Amin (former Ugandan dictator)

This chapter includes two cases which were brought by veterans and widows to recover compensation for injuries which were suffered in the line of duty. The Veterans' Benefit Act allows veterans and their survivors to apply for benefits, if the veteran is disabled or killed while serving his country. These awards are determined by the Veterans Administration (VA). The benefits are not overly generous. Because of this, many veterans, when they are injured by the government's misconduct, seek justice in the courts.

It is ironic that the Supreme Court would deny veterans the rights that they fought to defend. While the Supreme Court has ruled that those denied welfare benefits have the right to an attorney to represent them, the Supreme Court has denied veterans this same right. The court has also denied veterans the right to sue the government for damages, when civilians have that right.

Radiation Victims

Albert Maxwell, an American soldier in the Pacific Theater during World War II, was captured by the Japanese. As a prisoner of war, he was held captive in Japan, and was exposed to radiation from both the Nagasaki and Hiroshima atomic bombs. He contended that this wartime exposure caused the cancer that he suffered from. In addition, Maxwell claimed that the radiation effects had caused four of his five children to die of rare congenital abnormalities in early childhood. The Veterans Administration denied his claims.

Don Cordray was exposed to radiation during atomic testing while on duty with the Navy. Mr. Cordray contracted cancer and other ailments. His claim for benefits was denied by the Veterans Administration.

Reason Warehime served in the Pacific during World War II. He was assigned to the clean-up detail dispatched to Nagasaki after it was leveled by an atomic blast. He was also exposed to a large dose of radiation at an atomic test. His disability rating was lowered from one-hundred percent to sixty percent.

Doris Wilson is the widow of a veteran whose ship was contaminated with radiation and who died of cancer, as a result. Her claim for survivor's benefits was denied.

Reason Warehime, by Jim Lerager.   *Don Cordray, by Jim Lerager.*

Albert Maxwell, by Jim Lerager.   *James Stanley, courtesy of Mr. Stanley.*

Protecting Veterans' Rights

The Veterans' law limits the amount an attorney can charge for a claim for service-related injuries to ten dollars. This fee limitation originated in a Civil War era law (1862) which limited attorney's fees to five dollars. In 1864, the limit was increased to ten dollars, where it has remained. In 1864, the average soldier earned about $4.50 per week. In order to protect veterans against unscrupulous lawyers, Congress limited the amount that attorneys could earn to about two weeks' salary.

Albert Maxwell, Reason Warehime, Don Cordray and Doris Wilson all sought representation by attorneys, but could not find any willing to represent them for only ten dollars. The National Association of Radiation Survivors and the Swords to Plowshares Veterans Rights Organization joined these four individuals in a federal court challenge to the ten dollars attorney's fee limitation.

The Lower Court Ruling

In 1984, the case was heard by Judge Marilyn Hall Patel in federal court in San Francisco, California. Judge Patel ruled that the government's paternalistic interest in ensuring that veterans' benefits are not depleted by attorneys' fees does not overcome the veteran's right to be represented by counsel. The judge ruled that plaintiffs Maxwell, Warehime, Cordray and Wilson had a right to select an attorney at their expense and issued a nationwide injunction against the Veterans Administration.[1]

The court ruled, in granting a preliminary injunction, that the VA could no longer even mention the limitation on attorneys fees in any publication, form or regulation, and required the agency to post its ruling in a prominent location in every VA office in the nation.

Straight to the Supreme Court

Judge Patel's decision apparently angered the Justice Department, because it took the unusual step of appealing her order directly to the Supreme Court, sidestepping the court of appeals.

The Supreme Court decided to review the matter, even though the district court's decision was only a preliminary decision. The lower court did not rule that the limitation on attorneys' fees was unconstitutional: it ruled that after a full trial it was likely that the plaintiffs would be able to prove that the statute was unconstitutional.

The Supreme Court went beyond ruling on the appeal of the preliminary injunction and directly held that the statutory limitation on attorneys' fees was constitutional.[2] Justice O'Connor, although voting with the majority, stated that the majority should not have reached the merits of the constitutional question. Justice Sandra Day O'Connor stated that the injunction should have been dissolved, and the case returned to the lower court for a consideration of the entire case.

The court ruled that Congress had the power to regulate attorneys' fees, even if those fees were so low as to ensure that the veterans would not be represented by counsel. The court gave two reasons for its decision.

First, Congress could legislate to protect veterans from attorneys and from themselves, and second, Congress could seek to minimize the cost of administering the VA's programs.

Justice John Stevens, joined by Justices William Brennan and Thurgood Marshall, wrote a brilliant dissenting opinion. He stated:

> "The Court does not appreciate the value of individual liberty. It may well be true that in the vast majority of the cases a veteran does not need to employ a lawyer . . . .

> *   *   *

> Everyone agrees, however, that there are some complicated cases in which the services of a lawyer would be useful to the veteran, and indeed, would simplify the work of the agency by helping to organize the relevant facts and to identify the controlling issues.

> *   *   *

> The law that was enacted in 1864 to protect veterans from unscrupulous lawyers—those who charge excessive fees—effectively denied today's veteran access to *all* lawyers who charge reasonable fees for their services.

*   *   *

We are concerned with the individual's right to spend his own money to obtain the advice and assistance of independent counsel in advancing his claim against the Government.

*   *   *

In my view, regardless of the nature of the dispute between the sovereign [the government] and the citizen—whether it be a criminal trial, a proceeding to terminate parental rights, a claim for social security benefits, a dispute over welfare benefits, or a pension claim asserted by the widow of a soldier who was killed on the battlefield—the citizen's right to consult an independent lawyer and to retain that lawyer to speak on his behalf is an aspect of liberty that is priceless. It should not be bargained away on the notion that a totalitarian appraisal of the mass of claims processed by the Veterans' Administration does not identify an especially high probability of error.

Unfortunately, the reason for the Court's mistake today is all too obvious. It does not appreciate the value of individual liberty."

The Acid Test

In 1958, James B. Stanley was a master sergeant in the Army at Fort Knox, Kentucky, where he lived with his wife and children. He responded to a posted notice and volunteered to wear protective clothing and equipment to see how it would work when exposed to chemical weapons.

Stanley was transferred to the Army's Chemical Warfare Lab, at the Edgewood Arsenal in Aberdeen, Maryland, to take part in the testing. During his tenure at the Edgewood Arsenal, on four different occasions, Stanley was told to drink a clear liquid. Like a good soldier, Master Sergeant James Stanley did what he was told and asked no questions.

During this time, Stanley suffered hallucinations, periods of incoherence, servere personality changes and loss of memory. He began to beat his wife and children. After his violent episodes, he had no memory of them.

Unbeknownst to Stanley, he was being used as a guinea pig. The clear liquid contained a heavy dose of lysergic acid diethylamide, commonly known as LSD. LSD is a strong hallucinogenic drug which was the cause of Stanley's mental disorders. Stanley was not alone: the Army subjected 1,000 others to this LSD testing between 1955 and 1958.

The University of Maryland Medical School willingly participated in these LSD tests on humans. Many believe that the CIA was behind the testing, but the intelligence agency denies that it had anything to do with it. Maryland medical interns were used to administer the hidden drugs.

Stanley stayed in the Army until he was honorably discharged in 1969. Because of the violent personality he developed after the LSD tests, his wife divorced him.

The Letter

In 1975, Stanley received a letter from the Walter Reed Army Medical Center in Washington, D.C. The letter asked Stanley if he would participate in a follow-up study concerning the LSD testing that took place in 1958. Stanley was, understandably, extremely upset. He finally understood what had happened to him, his family and his mind. Because he was angry at what his government had done to him, and he sought justice in the courts.

He hired an attorney who sought additional details on the LSD testing program. The attorney applied for compensation, on Stanley's behalf, with both the Army and the CIA. The government stonewalled it. They would give Stanley nothing.

Finally, in 1978, Stanley filed suit in federal court in Florida against the Army and the Central Intelligence Agency for intentionally causing him harm and subjecting him to medical experimentation without his consent, and for failing to care for him after they gave him hallucinogenic drugs.

DEPARTMENT OF THE ARMY
WALTER REED ARMY INSTITUTE OF RESEARCH
WALTER REED ARMY MEDICAL CENTER
WASHINGTON, D.C. 20012

REPLY TO
ATTENTION OF:

SGRD-UWI-A

10 December 1975

Mr. James Bradley Stanley
345 Ponte Vedra Road
Palm Springs, Florida 33460

Dear Mr. Stanley:

According to our records, you were a participant in the chemical warfare
tests with lysergic acid diethylamide (LSD) conducted by the Biomedical
Laboratory, Edgewood Arsenal, Aberdeen Proving Ground, Maryland. Under
the auspices of the Surgeon General, a follow-up study of volunteers who
participated in these experiments will be conducted over the next two
years. We earnestly solicit your cooperation and participation in this
study.

The study will consist of providing all former participants with a
comprehensive medical examination at an Army Medical Center. Through
these examinations, we will attempt to first assess the overall health
status of former participants and, second, to determine whether there
have been any long-term aftereffects that might be traceable to participation in the LSD experiment.

If you have any questions, or if you would like to discuss the examination
or the study, please call the Medical Follow-Up Evaluation Group at
(202)427-5210 (call collect) and ask for Mrs. Sotzsky. If for any
reason you wish your appointment for examination in this follow-up study
to be at an earlier date, do not hesitate to contact Mrs. Sotzsky. She
will be pleased to either discuss the examination with you or provide
you access to a physician or other health professional who will be happy
to answer any questions you may have.

Our thanks for your consideration and cooperation.

Sincerely,

Harry C. Holloway

HARRY C. HOLLOWAY, M.D.
COL, MC
Dir, Division of Neuropsychiatry

Federal Court

Stanley's case bounced around the federal courts for nearly a decade. At first, Judge Gonzalez dismissed Stanley's case against the federal government. However, Gonzalez allowed him to add individual defendants to the case, including the University of Maryland and the doctors who administered the LSD to him.[3]

Judge Gonzalez stated:

> "There is a constitutional right to decide for oneself to submit to drug therapy.

> * * *

> This court views the conduct alleged . . . as an egregious intrusion on the most precious right protected by the Constitution—the right not to be deprived of life, liberty or property without due process of law."

The case was appealed to the court of appeals. The three-judge court, unanimously, ruled that Stanley could not only sue the individuals involved, but he also had the right to sue the United States government.[4] The court of appeals sent the case back for trial. However, before the case went back to the trial court, the government appealed.

At the Nation's Highest Court

The Supreme Court agreed to hear the case. On

June 25, 1987, just before this book went to press, the court issued its decision by a vote of five to four. Justice Antonin Scalia wrote the majority opinion in which he was joined by Justice Harry Blackmun, William Rehnquist, Byron White and Lewis Powell.

By the slimmest of majorities, the court ruled that the government was immune from suit by those who were in the military. According to the court, lawsuits of this type would interfere with military discipline. They ruled that it would be "inappropriate" for soldiers to be allowed to sue their superior officers. The court did not say what the effects of the suit would be on Army morale: our soldiers are being treated like second-class citizens and are being forced to give up their constitutional rights.

Justice O'Connor wrote a bitter dissent:

> "In my view, conduct of the type alleged in this case is so far beyond the bounds of human decency that as a matter of law it simply cannot be considered a part of the military mission . . . [and we] cannot insulate defendants from liability for deliberate and calculated exposure of otherwise healthy military personnel to medical experimentation without their consent, outside of any combat, combat training, or military exigency, and for no other reason than to gather information on the effect of lysergic acid diethylamide on human beings.

* * *

No judicially crafted rule should insu-
late from liability the involuntary and
unknowing human experimentation alleged to have occurred in this case."

Justices William Brennan, Thurgood Marshall and
John Stevens also dissented, vigorously. Their joint
dissenting opinion found that the Army had violated
the Nuremburg Code, regarding medical experimentation on human beings. They concluded that the actions
of the government were "serious violations of the constitutional rights of soldiers [that] must be exposed and
punished."

The result of the decision is that all of the defendants are immune from suit. The Supreme Court
cloaked the Army and all persons acting under their
"authority" with immunity. Had Germany won World
War II, lawsuits against the Reich would have been
treated in the same manner, and the Nuremburg Trials
would not have occurred. As the dissent stated, "soldiers
ought not be asked to defend a Constitution indifferent
to their essential human dignity."

Epilogue

The dissenting opinions in these two soldiers' rights
cases were joined by the court's liberal wing, which
now includes only Justices Brennan and Marshall. In
the *Stanley* case, they were joined by a moderate,

Justice Stevens, and by the court's relatively recent appointed conservative, Sandra Day O'Connor. Conservative columnist James J. Kilpatrick called the *Stanley* case "indefensible" and added, "Something is sorely wrong here." Justice Stevens, also, authored the dissenting opinion in the radiation victims case.

Only one of the radiation survivors, Reason Wareheim, is still alive. Mr. Cordray died while the case was at the court of appeals, and Mr. Maxwell died while waiting for the Supreme Court to rule. James Stanley has fared much better: he has now substantially recovered from the ill-effects of LSD. Since 1970, he has been a police officer with the Palm Beach County (Florida) police department. At age fifty-three, Stanley is healthy and has resumed contact with his ex-wife and daughters. However, he retains bitterness against the Army.

Although both of these cases denied remedies to members of our armed services and their families, the court arrived at its decision for different reasons. In the radiation victims case, the court upheld the constitutionality of an act of Congress which limited attorneys' fees to ten dollars.

In the *Stanley* case, the court was involved in creating its own exceptions to a federal statute. The court could have simply followed the statute and allowed Mr. Stanley compensation. However, as in other cases, the court refused to overrule its 1950 decision in the *Feres* case, which established the doctrine that soldiers could not recover damages against the government "for injuries that arise out of their military service." The court's tendency to follow earlier decisions has led to some of the nation's worst decisions.

Similarly, some of the longstanding statutes, like the one embodying the ten dollar limitation, have survived because they have been around so long. Sunday closing laws were also approved because they had been around for so long. But just because a law has been around for a hundred years or more does not make it good or constitutional. In fact, as Justice Stevens said concerning the ten dollar limit, time and inflation made the law unconstitutional.

Congress has the power to change both of these decisions. It is up to Congress to provide justice to the men and women who are responsible for defending our country.

Endnotes

1. 589 F.Supp. 1302 (1984).
2. 105 S.Ct. 3180 (1985).
3. 549 F.Supp 327.
4. 786 F.2d 1490 (April 21, 1986).
5. 483 U.S. 669 (June 25, 1987).

Chapter Twenty-Two

Mother Knows Best?

"Where law ends, tyranny begins."

—William Pitt

Linda Kay McFarlin dropped out of the public high school in Kendallville, Indiana, when she was sixteen. Kendallville is a town of about 8,000 people, located twenty-five miles away from Fort Wayne and tucked into the far northeast corner of Indiana, about a half-hour drive from either Ohio or Michigan. Linda was an average student and was never kept behind at school. But she was bored, so she left the DeKalb County High School and found a job to support herself.

It was then that she met Leo Sparkman. They fell in love and married after a short engagement. She was only seventeen when they married, and he was barely a year older.

The Mother

Linda's mother, Ora McFarlin, was happy when her daughter got engaged and gave her consent to the marriage. Linda had run away from home a lot when she was in her early teens. Sometimes, she had stayed out overnight, and her mother worried that she might come home pregnant one day. Mrs. McFarlin worked as a dishwasher at a nearby hospital and was relieved when Leo Sparkman married her daughter and took responsibility over her.

Leo and Linda Sparkman. Photograph by David Kurtz.

The Doctor

Linda and Leo Sparkman tried for three years to have children, without success. Disappointed, Linda asked her mother if she knew why they were infertile. Mrs. McFarlin told Linda that her fallopian tubes had been tied, but that she could have them untied if she desired to have children.

Linda could only recall having had one operation, an appendectomy five years earlier when she was fifteen-years-old. She went to see her family doctor, Dr. John Hines, who told her that he had, in fact, performed an appendectomy on her and had done nothing which would have affected her fertility.

Mrs. Sparkman and her husband didn't know whom they should believe, her mother or Dr. Hines. As far as Linda knew, Dr. Hines was the only one who had ever operated on her. And he said that he performed only an appendectomy. That is what he had told her five years earlier, and he told her the same thing again. But her mother told her that her tubes had been tied. One of them was lying.

The Lawyer

Linda and Leo Sparkman were determined to find out the truth. They made an appointment to see Richard Finley, one of the few lawyers in Kendallville. Mr. Finley wrote a letter to Dr. Hines, on behalf of the Sparkmans, asking him for details of the surgery that he performed on Mrs. Sparkman. In response to Mr. Finley's letter, Dr. Hines admitted the truth.

Hines admitted that he had performed a tubal ligation and that, as a result of the operation, Linda was sterile. He admitted that he never performed an appendectomy on Linda, but lied to her to conceal the true nature of the surgery. Dr. Hines stated that Ora McFarlin had received court approval for the operation and had agreed to indemnify him if there were "complications." These complications were just beginning.

Lawyer Finley drove to Auburn, Indiana, the county seat of DeKalb County, where the Circuit Court was located. He checked with the clerk's office. The clerk had no record of any lawsuit concerning either Ora or Linda McFarlin. The attorney checked further. After an exhaustive search Finley found a document entitled "Petition to have tubal libation performed on minor and indemnity agreement." The petition read as follows:

State of Indiana

County of DeKalb:

PETITION TO HAVE TUBAL LIGATION PERFORMED ON MINOR AND INDEMNITY AGREEMENT

Ora Spitler McFarlin, being duly sworn upon her oath states that she is the natural mother of and has custody of her daughter, Linda Spitler, age fifteen (15) being born January 24, 1956 and said daughter resides with her at 108 Iwo Street, Auburn, DeKalb County, Indiana.

Affiant states that her daughter's mentality is such that she is considered somewhat retard-

ed although she is attending or had attended
the public schools in DeKalb Central School
System and has been passing along with other
children in her age level even though she does
not have what is considered normal mental
capabilities and intelligence. Further, that said
affiant has had problems in the home of said
child as a result of said daughter leaving home
on several occasions to association with older
youth or young men and as a matter of fact
having stayed overnight with said youth or
men and about which incidents said affiant did
not become aware of until after such incidents
occurred. As a result of this behavior and the
mental capabilities of said daughter, affiant believes that it is to the best interest of said
child that a Tubal Ligation be performed on
said minor child to prevent unfortunate circumstances to occur and since it is impossible
for the affiant as mother of said chld to
maintain and control a continuous observation
of the activities of said daughter each and
every day.

Said affiant does hereby in consideration of
the Court of the DeKalb Circuit Court approv-
ing the Tubal Ligation being performed upon
her minor daughter hereby agree to indemnify
and keep indemnified and hold Dr. John Hines,
Auburn, Indiana, who said affiant is requesting
to perform said operation and DeKalb Memorial Hospital, Auburn, Indiana, where said
operation will be performed, harmless from
and against all or any matter or causes of
action that could or might arise as a result of

the performing of said Tubal Ligation.

In witness whereof, said affiant, Ora Spitler McFarlin, has hereunto subscribed her name this 9th day of July, 1971.

Signed: Ora Spitler McFarlin

The Judge

Mrs. McFarlin had appeared before Judge Harold Stump on the 9th of July, 1971, with her attorney. Judge Stump approved the order at once and signed his approval on the face of the petition. Linda McFarlin was neither present nor informed that her sterilization was being considered. In a case like this, where a parent seeks to have her child sterilized, most judges would appoint a guardian *ad litem*, a guardian for the purpose of that one case, to make sure that the interests of the child were considered. But this was not a normal case, and Judge Stump was not a very good judge. In violation of court procedures, Judge Stump did not even have the petition filed with the clerk's office. That is why Linda McFarlin's attorney had trouble finding it.

Judge Stump held no hearing on the petition. He did not notify anyone that the petition was going to be considered. There was no one present to cross-examine Mrs. McFarlin. Linda McFarlin's sterilization was approved by a judge on her mother's word, alone. And because no one else knew about the judge's decision, there could be no appeal.

Daughter Versus Mother

No one told Linda McFarlin what happened in the DeKalb County Circuit Court that day. No one told her that she was going to be sterilized. Not her mother. Not her doctor. Not Judge Stump. Her mother and her doctor lied to her. They told her that she was going to have her appendix removed.

On July 15, 1971, less than a week after Judge Stump's approval, Linda was admitted to DeKalb Memorial Hospital and she was irreversibly sterilized.

Understandably, the Sparkmans and their attorney, were furious. Attorney Finley promptly prepared the necessary court papers, and, on November 26, 1976, Linda and Leo Sparkman filed suit against Linda's mother, Judge Stump, Dr. Hines, an assisting doctor, the anesthesiologist and the hospital. Their attorney argued, before the federal court in Fort Wayne, that all of the defendants had conspired to deprive Linda Sparkman of her most valuable civil right, the right to have children.

The federal judge ruled against the Sparkmans, finding that judges are absolutely immune from such suits and that Judge Stump's approval of the sterilization gave the doctors and the hospital immunity, as well.

The Sparkmans appealed. The federal court of appeals for the area, that includes Indiana, is in Chicago and is called the United States Court of Appeals for the Seventh Circuit. Three judges are assigned to hear all federal appeals.

The court of appeals heard arguments in the case in January 1977, and made its decision that March. Unanimously, the judges ruled that Judge Stump had "no jurisdiction" when he ordered Linda McFarlin sterilized and that, therefore, he could be sued for damages. The court reasoned that judges were immune only from suits concerning actions taken within their authorized jurisdiction. And when judges act far beyond their authority, or outside of their jurisdiction, they are to be treated as ordinary citizens would be treated, with no immunity from lawsuits.

At last, it looked as though Linda Sparkman would receive some compensation, if only monetary, for the right that was taken away from her. But, then, Judge Harold Stump appealed the court of appeal's decision to the U.S. Supreme Court. The State of Indiana filed a brief in support of Judge Stump, arguing that judges must have absolute immunity, so that they will act without fear of retaliation. A little fear would have been good for Judge Stump. Maybe he wouldn't have ordered a teenage girl to be irreversibly sterilized, without notice or a hearing, had he feared that one day he could be sued for it. Maybe Judge Stump would have asked Linda McFarlin if she objected to her sterilization, and maybe, just maybe, Judge Stump would have appointed counsel to represent the minor child.

Several mental health organizations filed briefs with the Supreme Court, in support of Leo and Linda Sparkman. The American Civil Liberties Union, also, filed a brief in support of the Sparkmans.

The Supreme Court

The United States Supreme Court heard oral arguments in the case, in January 1978, and issued its ruling in March. The court ruled five to three, with Justice Brennan not voting, to reverse the decision of the court of appeals. They ruled that Judge Stump could not be sued, that he was absolutely immune from lawsuits concerning his actions as a judge.

Justice Byron White wrote the opinion for the majority of the court. He wrote that "because Judge Stump performed the type of act normally performed only by judges and because he did so in his capacity as a Circuit Court Judge, we find no merit to respondent's argument" that should deprive the judge of absolute immunity. Justice Potter Stewart, an Ohioan, dissented: "I think that what Judge Stump did on July 9, 1971, was beyond the pale of anything that could sensibly be called a judicial act."

The case was sent back to the court of appeals to determine whether the judge's immunity should shield the doctors and the hospital, as well as Ora McFarlin. The Court of Appeals ruled that all of the defendants were immune from suit and dismissed the case.

Epilogue

Linda Sparkman is still married to Leo Sparkman. They live together in Kendallville, not far from Mrs. McFarlin. However, the mother and daughter do not talk to each other any more.

Absolute immunity for judges is a court-made principle. It is not based on the Constitution of the United States, nor on a statute passed by Congress nor by state legislation. It, pure and simply, is made by judges, solely for judges. Federal judges have life tenure so that they can make their decisions without the fear that they will lose their judicial appointments. But, absolute judicial immunity can make judges into tyrants who cannot be questioned, except by appeal to a higher court. Absolute immunity places judges above the law. As we see from this case, they have the power to enforce, and to ignore, the law.

With ordinary cases, we do not want our judges to be sued because litigants are unhappy with the judges' decisions. In such a case, if a person disagrees with a judge's ruling, he or she can appeal it. However, with extraordinary cases, it may be in the interests of justice to seek to have a judge removed from office by complaining to a judicial review board. Federal judges can only be removed from office by Congressional impeachment proceedings, not the most effective route. Only three federal jurists have been removed by impeachment in the entire history of our republic.

Judge Stump's "order" was not an ordinary court decision. It was made "ex parte," which means that it was made with only one side being present. This is only allowed when an emergency prevents the other side from being notified, and, in such cases, decisions can only be temporary ones, lasting not more than ten days. And when this ten-day period expires, there must be a hearing to which both sides are invited.

Judge Stump made no effort to notify Linda McFarlin of the case against her, yet he ordered an irreversible operation to be performed. Judge Stump heard no testimony, allowed no examination of witnesses and deprived a young woman of due process, a fair hearing, the right to counsel, the right to cross-examine witnesses against her, the right to present witnesses on her behalf, and, worst of all, he deprived her of her natural and constitutional right to motherhood. This ruling, which gives Judge Stump, and all other judges, absolute immunity, should be changed by a constitutional amendment which gives judges only limited immunity. A statute along the same lines may be effective, but judges would have an opportunity to overturn such a statute. No court, not even the Supreme Court, can ignore or overturn an explicit constitutional amendment.

Endnotes

1. *Stump v. Sparkman*, 435 U.S. 349 (1978).

Appendix

Constitution of the United States

We the People of the United States, in Order to form a more perfect Union, establish Justice, insure domestic Tranquility, provide for the common defence, promote the general Welfare, and secure the Blessings of Liberty to ourselves and our Posterity, do ordain and establish this Constitution for the United States of America.

Article I.

Section 1. All legislative Powers herein granted shall be vested in a Congress of the United States, which shall consist of a Senate and House of Representatives.

Section 2. The House of Representatives shall be composed of Members chosen every second Year by the People of the several States, and the Electors in each State shall have the Qualifications requisite for Electors of the most numerous Branch of the State Legislature.

No Person shall be a Representative who shall not have attained to the Age of twenty five Years, and been seven Years a Citizen of the United States, and who shall not, when elected, be an Inhabitant of that State in which he shall be chosen.

[Representatives and direct Taxes shall be apportioned among the several States which may be included within this Union, according to their respective Numbers, which shall be determined by adding to the whole Number of free Persons, including those bound to Service for a Term of Years, and excluding Indians not taxed, three fifths of all other Persons.][1]

The actual Enumeration shall be made within three Years after the first Meeting of the Congress of the United States, and within every subsequent Term of ten Years, in such Manner as they shall by Law direct. The number of Representatives shall not exceed one for every thirty Thousand, but each State shall have at Least one Representative; and until such enumeration shall be made, the State of New Hampshire shall be entitled to chuse three, Massachusetts eight, Rhode-Island and Providence Plantations one, Connecticut five, New-York six, New Jersey four, Pennsylvania eight, Delaware one, Maryland six, Virginia ten, North Carolina five, South Carolina five, and Georgia three.

When vacancies happen in the Representation from any State, the Executive Authority thereof shall issue Writs of Election to fill such Vacancies.

The House of Representatives shall chuse their Speaker and other Officers; and shall have the sole Power of Impeachment.

Section 3. The Senate of the United States shall be composed of two Senators from each State, [chosen by the Legislature thereof,]2 for six Years; and each Senator shall have one Vote.

Immediately after they shall be assembled in Consequence of the first Election, they shall be divided as equally as may be into three Classes. The Seats of the Senators of the first Class shall be vacated at the Expiration of the second Year, of the second Class at the Expiration of the fourth Year, and of the third Class at the Expiration of the sixth Year, so that one third may be chosen every second Year; [and if Vacancies happen by Resignation, or otherwise, during the Recess of the Legislature of any State, the Executive thereof may make temporary Appointments until the next Meeting of the Legislature, which shall then fill such Vacancies.]3

No Person shall be a Senator who shall not have attained to the Age of thirty Years, and been nine Years a Citizen of the United States, and who shall not, when elected, be an Inhabitant of that State for which he shall be chosen.

The Vice President of the United States shall be President of the Senate, but shall have no Vote, unless they be equally divided.

The Senate shall chuse their other Officers, and also a President pro tempore, in the Absence of the Vice President, or when he shall exercise the Office of President of the United States.

The Senate shall have the sole Power to try all Impeachments. When sitting for that Purpose, they shall be on Oath or

Affirmation. When the President of the United States is tried, the Chief Justice shall preside: And no Person shall be convicted without the Concurrence of two thirds of the Members present.

Judgment in Cases of Impeachment shall not extend further than to removal from Office, and disqualification to hold and enjoy any Office of honor, Trust, or Profit under the United States: but the Party convicted shall nevertheless be liable to Indictment, Trial, Judgment and Punishment, according to Law.

Section 4. The Times, Places and Manner of holding Elections for Senators and Representatives, shall be prescribed in each State by the Legislature thereof; but the Congress may at any time by Law make or alter such Regulations, except as to the Places of chusing Senators.

The Congress shall assemble at least once in every Year, and such Meeting shall be [on the first Monday in December,]4 unless they shall by Law appoint a different Day.

Section 5. Each House shall be the Judge of the Elections, Returns and Qualifications of its own Members, and a Majority of each shall constitute a Quorum to do Business; but a smaller Number may adjourn from day to day, and may be authorized to compel the Attendance of absent Members, in such Manner, and under such Penalties as each House may provide.

Each House may determine the Rules of its Proceedings, punish its Members for disorderly Behaviour, and, with the Concurrence of two thirds, expel a Member.

Each House shall keep a Journal of its Proceedings, and from time to time publish the same, excepting such Parts as may in their Judgment require Secrecy; and the Yeas and Nays of the Members of either House on any question shall, at the Desire of one fifth of those Present, be entered in the Journal.

Neither House, during the Session of Congress, shall, without the Consent of the other, adjourn for more than three days, nor to any other Place than that in which the two Houses shall be sitting.

Section 6. The Senators and Representatives shall receive a Compensation for their Services, to be ascertained by Law, and paid out of the Treasury of the United States. They shall in all Cases, except Treason, Felony and Breach of the Peace, be privileged from Arrest during their Attendance at the Session of their respective Houses, and in going to and returning from the same; and for any Speech or Debate in either House, they shall not be questioned in any other Place.

No Senator or Representative shall, during the Time for which he was elected, be appointed to any civil Office under the Authority of the United States, which shall have been created, or the Emoluments whereof shall have been encreased during such time; and no Person holding any Office under the United States, shall be a Member of either House during his Continuance in Office.

Section 7. All Bills for raising Revenue shall originate in the House of Representatives; but the Senate may propose or concur with Amendments as on other Bills.

Every Bill which shall have passed the House of Representatives and the Senate, shall, before it becomes a Law, be presented to the President of the United States; If he approve he shall sign it, but if not he shall return it, with his Objections to that House in which it shall have originated, who shall enter the Objections at large on their Journal, and proceed to reconsider it. If after such Reconsideration two thirds of that House shall agree to pass the Bill, it shall be sent, together with the Objections, to the other House, by which it shall likewise be reconsidered, and if approved by two thirds of that House, it shall become a Law. But in all Cases the Votes of both Houses shall be determined by yeas and Nays, and the Names of the Persons voting for and against the Bill shall be entered on the Journal of each House respectively. If any Bill shall not be returned by the President within ten Days (Sundays excepted) after it shall have been presented to him, the Same shall be a Law, in like Manner as if he had signed it, unless the Congress by its Adjournment prevent its Return, in which case it shall not be a Law

Every Order, Resolution, or Vote to which the Concurrence of the Senate and House of Representatives may be necessary (except on a question of Adjournment) shall be presented to the President of the United States; and before the Same shall take Effect, shall be approved by him, or being disapproved by him, shall be repassed by two thirds of the Senate and House of Representatives, according to the Rules and Limitations prescribed in the Case of a Bill.

Section 8. The Congress shall have Power To lay and collect Taxes, Duties, Imposts and Excises, to pay the Debts and provide for the common Defence and general Welfare of the United States; but all Duties, Imposts and Excises shall be uniform throughout the United States;

To borrow Money on the credit of the United States;

To regulate Commerce with foreign Nations, and among the several States, and with the Indian Tribes;

To establish an uniform Rule of Naturalization, and uniform Laws on the subject of Bankruptcies throughout the United States;

To coin Money, regulate the Value thereof, and of foreign Coin, and fix the Standard of Weights and Measures;

To provide for the Punishment of counterfeiting the Securities and current Coin of the United States;

To establish Post Offices and post Roads;

To promote the Progress of Science and useful Arts, by securing for limited Times to Authors and Inventors the exclusive Right to their respective Writings and Discoveries;

To constitute Tribunals inferior to the supreme Court;

To define and punish Piracies and Felonies committed on the high Seas, and Offenses against the Law of Nations;

To declare War, grant Letters of Marque and Reprisal, and make Rules concerning Captures on Land and Water;

To raise and support Armies, but no Appropriation of Money to that Use shall be for a longer Term than two Years;

To provide and maintain a Navy;

To make Rules for the Government and Regulation of the land and naval Forces;

To provide for the calling forth of the Militia to execute the Laws of the Union, suppress Insurrections and repel Invasions;

To provide for organizing, arming, and disciplining, the Militia, and for governing such Part of them as may be employed in the Service of the United States, reserving to the States respectively, the Appointment of the Officers, and the authority of training the Militia according to the discipline prescribed by Congress;

To exercise exclusive Legislation in all Cases whatsoever, over such District (not exceeding ten Miles square) as may, by Cession of particular States, and the Acceptance of Congress, become the Seat of Government of the United States, and to exercise like Authority over all Places purchased by the Consent of the Legislature of the State in which the Same shall be, for the Erection of Forts, Magazines, Arsenals, dock-Yards, and other needful Buildings;—And

To make all Laws which shall be necessary and proper for carrying into Execution the foregoing Powers, and all other Powers vested by this Constitution in the Government of the United States, or in any Department or Officer thereof.

Section 9. The Migration or Importation of such Persons as any of the States now existing shall think proper to admit, shall not be prohibited by the Congress prior to the Year one thousand eight hundred and eight, but a Tax or duty may be imposed on such Importation, not exceeding ten dollars for each Person.

The Privilege of the Writ of Habeas Corpus shall not be suspended, unless when in Cases of Rebellion or Invasion the public Safety may require it.

No Bill of Attainder or ex post facto Law shall be passed.

No Capitation, or other direct, Tax shall be laid, unless in Proportion to the Census or Enumeration herein before directed to be taken.

No Tax or Duty shall be laid on Articles exported from any State.

No Preference shall be given by any Regulation of Commerce or Revenue to the Ports of one State over those of another: nor shall Vessels bound to, or from, one State, be obliged to enter, clear, or pay Duties in another.

No Money shall be drawn from the Treasury, but in Consequence of Appropriations made by Law; and a regular Statement and Account of the Receipts and Expenditures of all public Money shall be published from time to time.

No Title of Nobility shall be granted by the United States: And no Person holding any Office of Profit or Trust under them, shall, without the Consent of the Congress, accept of any present, Emolument, Office, or Title, of any kind whatever, from any King, Prince, or foreign State.

Section 10. No State shall enter into any Treaty, Alliance, or Confederation; grant Letters of Marque and Reprisal; coin Money; emit Bills of Credit; make any Thing but gold and silver Coin a Tender in Payment of Debts; pass any Bill of Attainder, ex post facto Law, or Law impairing the Obligation of Contracts, or grant any Title of Nobility.

No State shall, without the Consent of the Congress, lay any Imposts or Duties on Imports or Exports, except what may be absolutely necessary for executing it's inspection Laws: and the net Produce of all Duties and Imposts, laid by any State on Imports or Exports, shall be for the Use of the Treasury of the United States; and all such Laws shall be subject to the Revision and Controul of the Congress.

No State shall, without the Consent of the Congress, lay any Duty of Tonnage, keep Troops, or Ships of War in time of Peace, enter into any Agreement or Compact with another State, or with a foreign Power, or engage in War, unless actually invaded, or in such imminent Danger as will not admit of delay.

Article II.

Section 1. The executive Power shall be vested in a President of the United States of America. He shall hold his Office during the Term of four Years, and, together with the Vice President, chosen for the same Term, be elected, as follows

Each State shall appoint, in such Manner as the Legislature thereof may direct, a Number of Electors, equal to the whole Number of Senators and Representatives to which the State may be entitled in the Congress: but no Senator or Representative, or Person holding an Office of Trust or Profit under the United States, shall be appointed an Elector.

[The Electors shall meet in their respective States, and vote by Ballot for two Persons, of whom one at least shall not be an Inhabitant of the same State with themselves. And they shall make a List of all the Persons voted for, and of the Number of Votes for each; which List they shall sign and certify, and transmit sealed to the Seat of the Government of the United States, directed to the President of the Senate. The President of the Senate shall, in the Presence of the Senate and House of Representatives, open all the Certificates, and the Votes shall then be counted. The person having the greatest Number of Votes shall be the President, if such a Number be a majority of the whole Number of Electors appointed; and if there be more than one who have such Majority, and have an equal Number of Votes, then the House of Representatives shall immediately chuse by Ballot one of them for President; and if no Person have a Majority, then from the five highest on the List the said House shall in like Manner chuse the President. But in chusing the President, the Votes shall be taken by States, the Representation from each State having one Vote; A quorum for this Purpose shall consist of a Member or Members from two thirds of the States, and a Majority of all the States shall be necessary to a Choice. In every Case, after the Choice of the President, the Person having the greatest Number of Votes of the Electors shall be the Vice President. But if there should remain two or more who have equal Votes, the Senate shall chuse from them by Ballot the Vice President.]5

The Congress may determine the Time of chusing the Electors, and the Day on which they shall give their Votes; which Day shall be the same throughout the United States.

No Person except a natural born Citizen, or a Citizen of the

United States, at the time of the Adoption of this Constitution, shall be eligible to the Office of the President; neither shall any person be eligible to that Office who shall not have attained to the Age of thirty five Years, and been fourteen Years a Resident within the United States.

[In Case of the Removal of the President from Office, or of his Death, Resignation, or Inability to discharge the Powers and Duties of the said Office, the Same shall devolve on the Vice President, and the Congress may by Law provide for the Case of Removal, Death, Resignation or Inability, both of the President and Vice President, declaring what Officer shall then act as President, and such Officer shall act accordingly, until the Disability be removed, or a President shall be elected.]6

The President shall, at stated Times, receive for his Services, a Compensation, which shall neither be increased nor diminished during the Period for which he shall have been elected, and he shall not receive within that Period any other Emolument from the United States, or any of them.

Before he enter on the Execution of his Office, he shall take the following Oath or Affirmation:—"I do solemnly swear (or affirm) that I will faithfully execute the Office of President of the United States, and will to the best of my Ability, preserve, protect and defend the Constitution of the United States."

Section 2. The President shall be Commander in Chief of the Army and Navy of the United States, and of the Militia of the several States, when called into the actual Service of the United States; he may require the Opinion, in writing, of the principal Officer in each of the executive Departments, upon any Subject relating to the Duties of their respective Offices, and he shall have Power to grant Reprieves and Pardons for Offenses against the United States, except in Cases of Impeachment.

He shall have the Power, by and with the Advice and Consent of the Senate, to make Treaties, provided two thirds of the Senators present concur; and he shall nominate, and by and with the Advice and Consent of the Senate, shall appoint Ambassadors, other public Ministers and Consuls, Judges of the supreme Court, and all other Officers of the United States, whose Appointments are not herein otherwise provided for, and which shall be established by Law: but the Congress may by Law vest the Appointment of such inferior Officers, as they think proper, in the President alone, in the Courts of Law, or in the Heads of Departments.

The President shall have the Power to fill up all Vacancies

that may happen during the Recess of the Senate, by granting Commissions which shall expire at the End of their next Session.

Section 3. He shall from time to time give to the Congress Information on the State of the Union, and recommend to their Consideration such Measures as he shall judge necessary and expedient; he may, on extraordinary Occasions, convene both Houses, or either of them, and in Case of Disagreement between them, with Respect to the Time of Adjournment, he may adjourn them to such Time as he shall think proper; he shall receive Ambassadors and other public Ministers; he shall take Care that the Laws be faithfully executed, and shall Commission all the Officers of the United States.

Section 4. The President, Vice President, and all civil Officers of the United States, shall be removed from Office on Impeachment for, and Conviction of, Treason, Bribery, or other high Crimes and Misdemeanors.

Article III.

Section 1. The judicial Power of the United States, shall be vested in one supreme Court, and in such inferior Courts as the Congress may from time to time ordain and establish. The Judges, both of the supreme and inferior Courts, shall hold their Offices during good Behaviour, and shall, at stated Times, receive for their Services, a Compensation, which shall not be diminished during their Continuance in Office.

Section 2. The judicial Power shall extend to all Cases, in Law and Equity, arising under this Constitution, the Laws of the United States, and Treaties made, or which shall be made, under their Authority;—to all Cases affecting Ambassadors, other public Ministers and Consuls;—to all Cases of admiralty and maritime Jurisdiction;—to Controversies to which the United States shall be a Party;—to Controversies between two or more States; between a State and Citizens of another State;—between Citizens of different States—between Citizens of the same State claiming Lands under Grants of different States, and between a State, or the Citizens thereof, and foreign States, Citizens, or Subjects.

In all Cases affecting Ambassadors, other public Ministers and Consuls, and those in which a State shall be Party, the supreme Court shall have original Jurisdiction. In all the other Cases before mentioned, the supreme Court shall have appellate

Jurisdiction, both as to Law and Fact, with such Exceptions, and under such Regulations as the Congress shall make.

The Trial of all Crimes, except in Cases of Impeachment; shall be by Jury; and such Trial shall be held in the State where the said Crimes shall have been committed; but when not committed within any State, the Trial shall be at such Place or Places as the Congress may by Law have directed.

Section 3. Treason against the United States, shall consist only in levying War against them, or in adhering to their Enemies, giving them Aid and Comfort. No Person shall be committed of Treason unless on the Testimony of two Witnesses to the same overt Act, or on Confession in open Court.

The Congress shall have Power to declare the Punishment of Treason, but no Attainder of Treason shall work Corruption of Blood, or Forfeiture except during the Life of the Person attainted.

Article IV.

Section 1. Full Faith and Credit shall be given in each State to the public Acts, Records, and judicial Proceedings of every other State; And the Congress may by general Laws prescribe the Manner in which such Acts, Records and Proceedings shall be proved, and the Effect thereof.

Section 2. The Citizens of each State shall be entitled to all Privileges and Immunities of Citizens in the several States.

A Person charged in any State with Treason, Felony, or other Crime, who shall flee from Justice, and be found in another State, shall on Demand of the executive Authority of the State from which he fled, be delivered up, to be removed to the State having Jurisdiction of the Crime.

[No person held to Service or Labour in one State, under the Laws thereof, escaping into another, shall, in Consequence of any Law or Regulation therein, be discharged from such Service or Labour, but shall be delivered up on Claim of the Party to whom such Service or Labour may be due.][7]

Section 3. New States may be admitted by the Congress into this Union; but no new State shall be formed or erected within the Jurisdiction of any other State; nor any State be formed by the Junction of two or more States, or Parts of States, without the Consent of the Legislatures of the States concerned as well as of the Congress.

The Congress shall have Power to dispose of and make all needful Rules and Regulations respecting the Territory or other Property belonging to the United States; and nothing in this Constitution shall be so construed as to Prejudice any Claims of the United States, or of any particular State.

Section 4. The United States shall guarantee to every State in this Union a Republican Form of Government, and shall protect each of them against Invasion; and on Application of the Legislature, or of the Executive (when the Legislature cannot be convened) against domestic Violence.

Article V.

The Congress, whenever two thirds of both Houses shall deem it necessary, shall propose Amendments to this Constitution, or, on the Application of the Legislatures of two thirds of the several States, shall call a Convention for proposing Amendments, which, in either Case, shall be valid to all Intents and Purposes, as Part of this Constitution, when ratified by the Legislatures of three fourths of the several States, or by Conventions in three fourths thereof, as the one or the other Mode of Ratification may be proposed by the Congress; Provided that no Amendment which may be made prior to the Year One thousand eight hundred and eight shall in any Manner affect the first and fourth Clauses in the Ninth Section of the first Article; and that no State, without its Consent, shall be deprived of it's equal Suffrage in the Senate.

Article VI.

All Debts contracted and Engagements entered into, before the Adoption of this Constitution, shall be as valid against the United States under this Constitution, as under the Confederation.

This Constitution, and the Laws of the United States which shall be made in Pursuance thereof; and all Treaties made, or which shall be made, under the Authority of the United States, shall be the supreme Law of the Land; and the Judges in every State shall be bound thereby, any Thing in the Constitution or Laws of any State to the Contrary notwithstanding.

The Senators and Representatives before mentioned, and the Members of the several State Legislatures, and all executive and judicial Officers, both of the United States and of the several States, shall be bound by Oath or Affirmation, to support this Constitution; but no religious Test shall ever be required as a Qualification to any Office or public Trust under the United States.

Article VII.

The Ratification of the Conventions of nine States, shall be sufficient for the Establishment of this Constitution between the States so ratifying the Same.

done in Convention by the Unanimous Consent of the States present the Seventeenth Day of September in the Year of our Lord one thousand eight hundred and Eighty seven and of the Independence of the United States of America the Twelfth In Witness whereof We have hereunto subscribed our Names,

G.° Washington—Presid.ᵗ
and deputy from Virginia

New Hampshire John Langdon
Nicholas Gilman

Massachusetts Nathaniel Gorham
Rufus King

Connecticut Wm. Saml. Johnson
Roger Sherman

New York Alexander Hamilton

New Jersey Wil: Livingston
David Brearley
Wm. Paterson
Jona: Dayton

Pennsylvania B Franklin
Thomas Mifflin
Robt Morris
Geo. Clymer
Thos. FitzSimons
Jared Ingersoll
James Wilson

Gouv Morris

Delaware Geo: Read
Gunning Bedford jun
John Dickinson
Richard Bassett
Jaco: Broom

Maryland James McHenry
Dan of St Thos. Jenifer
Danl Carroll

Virginia John Blair—
James Madison Jr.

North Carolina Wm. Blount
Richd. Dobbs Spaight
Hu Williamson

South Carolina J. Rutledge
Charles Cotesworth Pinckney
Charles Pinckney
Pierce Butler

Georgia William Few
Abr Baldwin

Attest William Jackson Secretary

AMENDMENTS

Amendment I.

Congress shall make no law respecting an establishment of religion, or prohibiting the free exercise thereof; or abridging the freedom of speech, or of press, the right of the people peaceably to assemble, and petition the Government for a redress of grievances.

Amendment II.

A well regulated Militia, being necessary to the security of a free State, the right of the people to keep and bear Arms, shall not be infringed.

Amendment III.

No Soldier shall, in time of peace be quartered in any house, without the consent of the Owner, nor in time of war, but in a manner to be prescribed by law.

Amendment IV.

The right of the people to be secure in their persons, houses, papers, and effects, against unreasonable searches and seizures, shall not be violated, and no Warrants shall issue, but upon probable cause, supported by Oath or affirmation, and particularly describing the place to be searched, and the persons or things to be seized.

Amendment V.

No person shall be held to answer for a capital, or otherwise infamous crime, unless on a presentment or indictment of a Grand Jury, except in cases arising in the land or naval forces, or in the Militia, when in actual service in time of War or public danger; nor shall any person be subject for the same offence to be twice put in jeopardy of life or limb, nor shall be compelled in any criminal case to be a witness against himself, nor be deprived of life, liberty, or property, without due process of law; nor shall private property be taken for public use without just compensation.

Amendment VI.

In all criminal prosecutions, the accused shall enjoy the right to a speedy and public trial, by an impartial jury of the State and district wherein the crime shall have been committed; which district shall have been previously ascertained by law, and to be informed of the nature and cause of the accusation; to be confronted with the witnesses against him; to have compulsory process for obtaining witnesses in his favor, and to have the assistance of counsel for his defence.

Amendment VII.

In Suits at common law, where the value in controversy shall exceed twenty dollars, the right of trial by jury shall be preserved, and no fact tried by a jury shall be otherwise re-examined in any Court of the United States, than according to the rules of the common law.

Amendment VIII.

Excessive bail shall not be required, nor excessive fines imposed, nor cruel and unusual punishments inflicted.

Amendment IX.

The enumeration in the Constitution of certain rights shall not be construed to deny or disparage others retained by the people.

Amendment X.

The powers not delegated to the United States by the Constitution, nor prohibited by it to the States, are reserved to the States respectively, or to the people.[8]

Amendment IX.

The enumeration in the Constitution of certain rights shall not be construed to deny or disparage others retained by the people.

Amendment X.

The powers not delegated to the United States by the Constitution, nor prohibited by it to the States, are reserved to the States respectively, or to the people.[8]

Amendment XI.

The judicial power of the United States shall not be construed to extend to any suit in law or equity, commenced or prosecuted against one of the United States by Citizens of another State, or by Citizens or Subjects of any Foreign State.[9]

Amendment XII.

The Electors shall meet in their respective states, and vote by ballot for President and Vice President, one of whom, at least, shall not be an inhabitant of the same state with themselves; they shall name in their ballots the person voted for as President, and in distinct ballots the person voted for as Vice-President, and they shall make distinct lists of all persons voted for as President, and all persons voted for as Vice-President, and of the number of votes for each, which lists they shall sign and certify, and transmit sealed to the seat of the government of the United States, directed to the President of the Senate;—The President of the Senate shall, in the presence of the Senate and House of Representatives, open all the certificates and the votes shall then be counted;—The person having the greatest number of votes for President, shall be the President, if such number be a majority of the whole number of Electors appointed; and if no person have such majority, then from the persons having the highest numbers not exceeding three on the list of those voted for as President, the House of Representatives shall choose immediately, by ballot, the President. But in choosing the President, the votes shall be taken by states, the representation from each state having one vote; a quorum for this purpose shall consist of a member or members from two-thirds of the states, and a majority of all the states shall be necessary to a choice. [And if the House of Representatives shall not choose a President whenever the right of choice shall devolve upon them, before the fourth day of March next following, then the Vice-President shall act as President, as in the case of the death or other constitutional disability of the President][10] The person having the greatest number of votes as Vice-President, shall be the Vice-President, if such number be a majority of the whole number of Electors appointed, and if no person have a majority, then from the two highest numbers on the list, the Senate shall choose the Vice-President; a quorum for the purpose shall consist of two-thirds of the whole number of Senators, and a majority of the whole number shall be necessary to a choice. But no person constitutionally ineligible to the office of President shall be eligible to that of Vice-President of the United States.[11]

Amendment XIII.

Section 1. Neither slavery nor involuntary servitude, except as a punishment for crime whereof the party shall have been duly convicted, shall exist within the United States, or any place subject to their jurisdiction.

Section 2. Congress shall have power to enforce this article by appropriate legislation.[12]

Amendment XIV.

Section 1. All persons born or naturalized in the United States and subject to the jurisdiction thereof, are citizens of the United States and of the State wherein they reside. No State shall make or enforce any law which shall abridge the privileges or immunities of citizens of the United States; nor shall any State deprive any person of life, liberty, or property, without due process of law; nor deny to any person within its jurisdiction the equal protection of the laws.

Section 2. Representatives shall be apportioned among the several States according to their respective numbers, counting the whole number of persons in each State, excluding Indians not taxed. But when the right to vote at each election for the choice of electors for President and Vice President of the United States, Representatives in Congress, the Executive and Judicial officers of a State, or the members of the Legislature thereof, is denied to any of the male inhabitants of such State, being twenty-one years of age, and citizens of the United Stets, or in any way abridged, except for participation in rebellion, or other crime, the basis of representation therein shall be reduced in the proportion which the number of such male citizens shall bear to the whole number of male citizens twenty-one years of age in such State.

Section 3. No person shall be a Senator or Representative in Congress, or elector of President and Vice President, or hold any office, civil or military, under the United States, or under any State, who, having previously taken an oath, as a member of Congress, or as an officer of the United States, or as a member of any State legislature, or as an executive or judicial officer of any State, to support the Constitution of the United States, shall have engaged in insurrection or rebellion against the same, or given aid and comfort to the enemies thereof. But Congress may by a vote of two-thirds of each House, remove such disability.

Section 4. The validity of the public debt of the United States, authorized by law, including debts incurred for payment of pensions and bounties for services in suppressing insurrection or rebellion, shall not be questioned. But neither the United States nor any State shall assume or pay any debt or obligation incurred in aid of insurrection or rebellion against the United States, or any claim for the loss or emancipation of any slave; but all such debts, obligations, and claims shall be held illegal and void.

Section 5. The Congress shall have power to enforce, by appropriate legislation, the provisions of this article.[13]

Amendment XV.

Section 1. The rights of citizens of the United States shall not be denied or abridged by the United States or by any State on account of race, color, or previous condition of servitude.

Section 2. The Congress shall have power to enforce this article by appropriate legislation.[14]

Amendment XVI.

The Congress shall have the power to lay and collect taxes on incomes, from whatever source derived, without apportionment among the several states, and without regard to any census or enumeration.[15]

Amendment XVII.

The Senate of the United States shall be composed of two Senators from each State, elected by the people thereof, for six years; and each Senator shall have one vote. The electors in each State shall have the qualifications requisite for electors of the most numerous branch of the State legislatures.

When vacancies happen in the representation of any State in the Senate, the executive authority of each State shall issue writs of election to fill such vacancies: *Provided,* That the legislature of any State may empower the executive thereof to make temporary appointments until the people fill the vacancies by election as the legislature may direct.

This amendment shall not be so construed as to affect the election or term of any Senator chosen before it becomes valid as part of the Constitution.[16]

Amendment XVIII.

[*Section 1.* After one year from the ratification of this article the manufacture, sale, or transportation of intoxicating liquors within, the importation thereof into, or the exportation thereof from the United States and all territory subject to the jurisdiction thereof for beverage purposes is hereby prohibited.

Section 2. The Congress and the several States shall have concurrent power to enforce this article by appropriate legislation.

Section 3. This article shall be inoperative unless it shall have been ratified as an amendment to the Constitution by the legislatures of the several States, as provided in the Constitution, within seven years from the date of the submission hereof to the States by the Congress.][17]

Amendment XIX.

The right of citizens of the United States to vote shall not be denied or abridged by the United States or by any State on account of sex.

Congress shall have power to enforce this article by appropriate legislation.[18]

Amendment XX.

Section 1. The terms of the President and Vice President shall end at noon on the 20th day of January, and the terms of Senators and Representatives at noon on the 3d day of January, of the years in which such terms would have ended if this article had not been ratified; and the terms of their successors shall then begin.

Section 2. The Congress shall assemble at least once in every year, and such meeting shall begin at noon on the 3d day of January, unless they shall by law appoint a different day.

Section 3. If, at the time fixed for the beginning of the term of the President, the President elect shall have died, the Vice President elect shall become President. If a President shall not have been chosen before the time fixed for the beginning of his term, or if the President elect shall have failed to qualify, then the Vice President elect shall act as President until a President shall have qualified; and the Congress may by law provide for the case wherein neither a President elect or a Vice President elect shall have qualified, declaring who shall then act as President, or the manner in which one who is to act shall be selected, and such person shall act accordingly until a President or Vice President shall have qualified.

Section 4. The Congress may by law provide for the case of the death of any of the persons from whom the House of Representatives may choose a President whenever the right of choice shall have devolved upon them, and for the case of the death of any of the persons from whom the Senate may choose a Vice President whenever the right of choice shall have devolved upon them.

Section 5. Sections 1 and 2 shall take effect on the 15th day of October following the ratification of this article.

Section 6. This article shall be inoperative unless it shall have been ratified as an amendment to the Constitution by the legislatures of three-fourths of the several States within seven years from the date of the submission.[19]

Amendment XXI.

Section 1. The eighteenth article of amendment to the Constitution of the United States is hereby repealed.

Section 2. The transportation or importation into any State,

Territory, or possession of the United States for delivery or use therein of intoxicating liquors, in violation of the laws thereof, is hereby prohibited.

Section 3. This article shall be inoperative unless it shall have been ratified as an amendment to the Constitution by conventions in the several States, as provided in the Constitution, within seven years from the date of submission hereof to the States by the Congress.[20]

Amendment XXII.

Section 1. No person shall be elected to the office of the President more than twice, and no person who has held the office of President, or acted as President, for more than two years of a term to which some other person was elected President shall be elected to the office of the President more than once. But this article shall not apply to any person holding the office of President when this article was proposed by the Congress, and shall not prevent any person who may be holding the office of President, or acting as President, during the term within which this article becomes operative from holding the office of President during the remainder of such term.

Section 2. This article shall be inoperative unless it shall have been ratified as an amendment to the Constitution by the legislatures of three-fourths of the several states within seven years from the date of its submission to the States by the Congress.[21]

Amendment XXIII.

Section 1. The District constituting the seat of Government of the United States shall appoint in such manner as the Congress may direct:

A number of electors of President and Vice President equal to the whole number of Senators and Representatives in Congress to which the District would be entitled if it were a State, but in no event more than the least populous State; they shall be in addition to those appointed by the States, but they shall be considered, for the purposes of election of President and Vice President, to be electors appointed by a State; and they shall meet in the District and perform such duties as provided by the twelfth article of amendment.

Section 2. The Congress shall have power to enforce this article by appropriate legislation.[22]

Amendment XXIV.

Section 1. The right of citizens of the United States to vote in any primary or other election for President or Vice President, for electors for President or Vice President, or for Senator or Representative in Congress, shall not be denied or abridged by the United States or any State by reason of failure to pay any poll tax or other tax.

Section 2. Congress shall have power to enforce this article by appropriate legislation.[23]

Amendment XXV.

Section 1. In case of the removal of the President from office or his death or resignation, the Vice President shall become President.

Section 2. Whenever there is a vacancy in the office of the Vice President, the President shall nominate a Vice President who shall take office upon confirmation by a majority vote of both Houses of Congress.

Section 3. Whenever the President transmits to the President pro tempore of the Senate and the Speaker of the House of Representatives his written declaration that he is unable to discharge the powers and duties of his office, and until he transmits to them a written declaration to the contrary, such powers and duties shall be discharged by the Vice President as Acting President.

Section 4. Whenever the Vice President and a majority of either the principal officers of the executive departments or of such other body as Congress may by law provide, transmit to the President pro tempore of the Senate and the Speaker of the House of Representatives their written declaration that the President is unable to discharge the powers and duties of his office, the Vice President shall immediately assume the powers and duties of the office as Acting President.

Thereafter, when the President transmits to the President pro tempore of the Senate and the Speaker of the House of Representatives his written declaration that no inability exists, he shall resume the powers of his office unless the Vice

President and a majority of the principal officers of the executive department or of such other body as Congress may by law provide, transmit within four days to the President pro tempore of the Senate and the Speaker of the House of Representatives their written declaration that the President is unable to discharge the powers and duties of his office. Thereupon Congress shall decide the issue, assembling within forty-eight hours for that purpose if not in session. If the Congress, within twenty-one days after receipt of the latter written declaration, or, if Congress is not in session, within twenty-one days after Congress is required to assemble, determines by two-thirds vote of both Houses that the President is unable to discharge the powers and duties of his office, the Vice President shall continue to discharge the same as Acting President; otherwise, the President shall resume the powers and duties of his office.[24]

Amendment XXVI.

Section 1. The right of Citizens of the United States, who are eighteen years of age or older, to vote shall not be denied or abridged by the United States or by any State on account of age.

Section 2. The Congress shall have power to enforce this article by appropriate legislation.[25]

Endnotes

1. Changed by section 2 of the Fourteenth Amendment.

2. Changed by the Seventeenth Amendment.

3. Changed by the Seventeenth Amendment.

4. Changed by section 2 of the Twentieth Amendment.

5. Superseded by the Twelfth Amendment.

6. Modified by the Twenty-Fifth Amendment.

7. Superseded by the Thirteenth Amendment.

8. The first ten Amendments (Bill of Rights) were ratified effective December 15, 1791.

9. The Eleventh Amendment was ratified February 7, 1795.

10. The Twelfth Amendment was ratified June 15, 1804.

11. Superseded by section 3 of the Twentieth Amendment.

12. The Thirteenth Amendment was ratified December 6, 1865.

13. The Fourteenth Amendment was ratified July 9, 1868.

14. The Fifteenth Amendment was ratified February 3, 1870.

15. The Sixteenth Amendment was ratified February 3, 1913.

16. The Seventeenth Amendment was ratified April 8, 1913.

17. The Eighteenth Amendment was ratified January 16, 1919. It was repealed by the Twenty-First Amendment.

18. The Nineteenth Amendment was ratified August 18, 1920.

19. The Twentieth Amendment was ratified January 23, 1933.

20. The Twenty-First Amendment was ratified December 5, 1933.

21. The Twenty-Second Amendment was ratified February 27, 1951.

22. The Twenty-Third Amendment was ratified March 29, 1961.

23. The Twenty-Fourth Amendment was ratified January 23, 1964.

24. The Twenty-Fifth Amendment was ratified February 10, 1967.

25. The Twenty-Sixth Amendment was ratified July 1, 1971.

Index